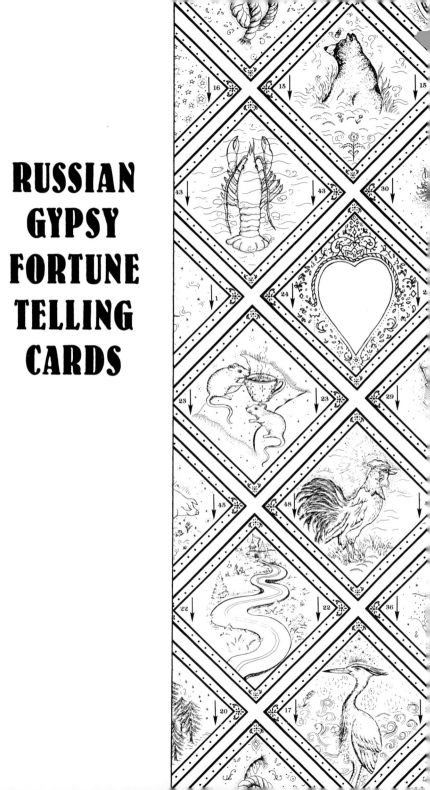

RUSSIAN GYPSY FORTUNE TELLING CARDS

RUSSIAN GYPSY FORTUNE TELLING CARDS

Svetlana
Alexandrovna
Touchkoff

HarperSanFrancisco
A Division of HarperCollins*Publishers*

OTHER TITLES OF INTEREST FROM HARPER SAN FRANCISCO

Sacred Path Cards: The Discovery of Self Through Native Teachings, by Jamie Sams

The Power Deck: The Cards of Wisdom, by Lynn V. Andrews

Book design by Sheree L. Goodman
Produced by 2M Communications Ltd.

FIRST EDITION

Library of Congress Cataloging-in-Publication Data

Touchkoff, Svetlana.
    Russian Gypsy fortune telling cards / Svetlana Alexandrovna Touchkoff.—1st ed.
        p.   cm.
    ISBN 0-06-250876-8
    1. Fortune-telling by cards. I. Title.
    BF1878.T683   1992
133.3'242'08991497047—dc20   90-56459
                                                     CIP

93 94 95 HCP–HK 10 9 8 7 6 5 4 3 2

This book is dedicated to
my mother,
Veronica Victorovna Touchkoff

I would like to thank my family, in particular my husband, for the support they have given me over the years in pursuing my dream. I would also like to thank all my friends who have shared my interest in the cards. And a special thanks goes to the Oakridge girls, for their encouragement, advice, and friendship.

CONTENTS

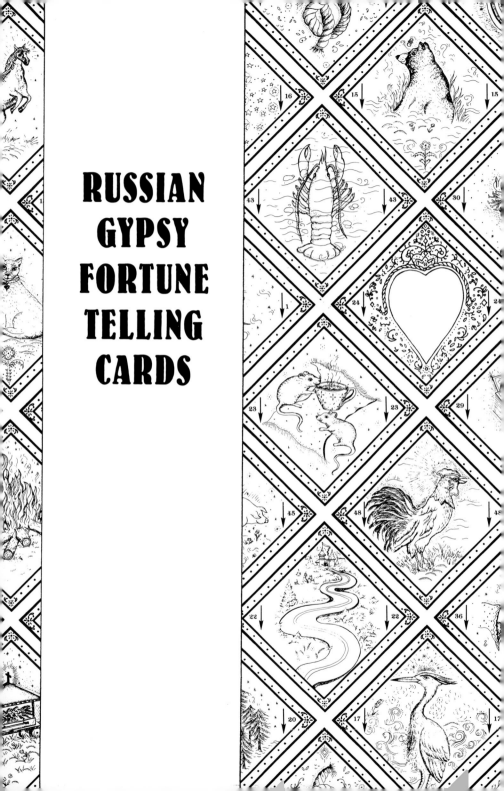

RUSSIAN
GYPSY
FORTUNE
TELLING
CARDS

PART I

HOW TO USE THE CARDS AND BOOK

INTRODUCTION

Fortune telling was once an integral part of people's lives in Russia, especially before 1917. During the week they told fortunes, while on Sundays they went to church and prayed. Everyone in the house participated. One person would do a reading, while the rest of the family or friends would sit around the table, listen, and make contributions. This was a time before table games or encounter sessions were developed. People wanted to have their fortunes told because it was a time they could concentrate on themselves, talk about their feelings or frustrations, and formulate strategies for the future. It was generally a happy time with everyone participating. The people believed in the predictions, yet they were not controlled by them. An individual's free will or God's intercession could turn any situation around. This open attitude by the Russian people toward fortune telling and the psychic world has remained to this day.

In Western society, people also have sought to understand the many forces inside and outside of them. Areas of specialization have developed. Astrology, numerology, and palmistry deal with the interpretation of outside forces, while psychology and dream interpretation try to unravel the inner or subconscious mind. Over the many centuries that these methods have been used, our understanding of

3

how people function has increased greatly. However, by becoming areas of specialization, these methods have become less accessible to the average person. In fact, fortune telling and psychology have split into two totally separate areas; fortune telling is considered quackery and psychology a science. During the last few decades, people who looked for help from either of these fields were considered odd or sick. Only recently have people started to become aware that the more they know about themselves, the more they can control their destinies. Information from various sources, including the psychic world, can help them to be the best that they can be.

Events over which we have very little or no control occur all the time. Weather conditions change; businesses collapse; car accidents, romances, and affairs occur; there are wars among nations; and we get sick. Even if we can predict an occurrence, it is difficult to prevent our physical and emotional reactions to it; nor should we try to. To have the power to predict and control our reactions to events would make robots of us. Our world would be safe but unfulfilled. Even God gave Adam and Eve the right to choose for themselves. Strong people have always fought for the right to choose, while despots have sought to control their actions.

The Russian Gypsy Fortune Telling Cards have the mystical power of predicting events, of indicating favorable and unfavorable circumstances. They can help us by revealing the situation, by making us aware, and by enabling us to choose the qualities that we should put forth to meet the situation. Yet, the cards do not seek to control us. How we see events and react to them is left to our own free will.

The cards are like a psychic barometer, naming for us the vibrations that surround us constantly.

In nature there are cycles such as day and night; summer, fall, winter, and spring; calm periods and storms. None of these natural phenomena are good or bad in themselves, but taken all together, they make up our universe. A flood can cause havoc by washing away houses and roads, yet it leaves behind silt that enriches the soil. If we had too much of one thing—for example, daylight—the earth would burn up. Thus in nature there are an order and a disorder that make up the whole.

The same thing applies to our lives. There is order in that we go through the stages of birth, childhood, adulthood, old age, and death. There is also disorder in that we go through bad and good periods, excitement, boredom, and many unpredictable circumstances. But as

4

in nature, these are all aspects of life that give it meaning. If we have too much prosperity, we grow lazy, or if we have too much strife or stress, we become sick. Therefore, we must learn to live with the changes in our lives and use them to our advantage.

Pilots check out the weather conditions before takeoff. They know their desired destination, but they fly the safest route. On very rare occasions lightning might strike the plane, but even then the crew is prepared for an emergency. Plane crashes generally are not caused by natural phenomena, but by human error in the maintenance or flying of the aircraft.

By doing a card reading, we are reading our psychic barometer. Are storms brewing for us, or is there smooth sailing ahead? Will our plans meet with success or failure? Is love, money, or travel favored at this time or not? Like pilots using the weather report to their best advantage, so we can use the cards to our best advantage. If it is a favorable time, we can enjoy it to its utmost; if it is an unfavorable time, we can brace ourselves for the storm and wait it out. Like the pilot, we cannot avoid all the storms, but we can minimize our losses. In fact, we can even enjoy the stormy periods, like the surfer who enjoys the challenge of the large waves, which would drown most of us.

My own life has been affected by the cards. I began using them in my late teens. At that time I was afraid of them because the HEARSE card kept coming up for me all the time, warning me of serious illness or death. I also had what seemed to be a short life line on my palm. I stopped using the cards, thinking that by avoiding the issue I would somehow escape the imminent death that I saw. Then when I was twenty-one, my legs began to go numb, and I lost control of my bladder and bowel functions. Still I avoided going to the doctor, hoping it would go away. Finally I had to go to my doctor as I could no longer walk. A nonmalignant tumor was found in my spine. I was rushed to the operating table, and five hours later, was free of the growth. Miraculously, the next time I did the cards, the HEARSE card did not appear. This was my first insight into the positive powers that the cards hold. They were there to warn me of danger, not to predict my demise. Had I gone to the doctor earlier, I would have had a much easier year and spared myself the embarrassment of not being in control of my body functions.

Over the years, the cards have come to my rescue innumerable times. They have crystallized into pictures that which I was feeling but unable to put into words. They also have shown me dangers that lay in my path. When we have problems, we quite often develop tunnel vision, seeing only our hurts. The cards reveal a larger picture. Doing a reading sometimes helps you realize that the problem is not of your creating and is unsolvable at this time. At other times, the cards will tell you that you have been complacent and negligent yourself. The cards have a way of calling out or bringing forth the best in you and guiding you to a positive solution of your problem.

The pictures on the cards are symbols or metaphors for our reality. When we see the picture, the mind transcends itself, extends itself beyond the conscious level. We remember more and put into practice more. We are using synergistic energy, an energy that combines the conscious and unconscious thoughts to make a stronger whole. Often just by seeing the pictures, we know what they refer to without having to read the meaning for the card. In the same way solutions will come for any problems we' may have.

The cards are a tool that can help us. Learning to use them is like learning a new language. When you learn a new language, it opens up a whole new world of experiences and people to you. In the same way, the cards help us to understand a whole new dimension of being. We don't have to follow the advice given, but when we do, it can be a great help in navigating our life.

People in the Western societies have forgotten how to get in touch with the center of their being, to trust their own instincts. Some of us pray, but we seldom thank God for giving us the power to control our lives. Instead, we ask for God's help in solving our dilemmas. Some people have turned to the Eastern cultures in their search to understand themselves by using yoga and meditation. The techniques work, but it is often difficult in our Western culture to find the time to practice the methods.

This is where the Russian Gypsy Fortune Telling Cards can be a useful method to us in the Western world. You can do a reading by yourself or with a group of friends or family members anytime, anywhere. It is a time when you can concentrate on yourself. The cards give you a reading of the major and minor movements or occurrences in your life. You can spend as much time as you want interpreting the reading. If you want to know one thing, the reading can take a few minutes and you are ready to proceed. If you are with a group of friends, their input into the reading can also be interesting and helpful. Some of my best readings and most enjoyable times have been when I was together with my friends or family members. The cards will stimulate a discussion that can go on for hours. By talking over the problems the cards point out with our friends or family, we come to a new understanding of ourselves and each other.

Every time I do a reading, I learn something new about myself or how the cards work. I have tried to summarize my experience from years of using the cards in the following pages of this book. The explanations will help you understand the meaning of the cards that come up for you. However, only your continual use of the cards will teach you what the particular cards refer to in your life. You don't have to use the cards all the time, but you will find that each time you use them, you will gain a greater understanding of the positive powers that they bring forth in you.

Origin of the Cards

The cards are derived from the Gypsy aspect of Russian folklore, and are a blend of animal, natural, and Christian symbols. The cards originated in the southwestern part of Russia where the Gypsies lived. The area was close to many civilizations: European, Slavic, Byzantine, Islamic, Indian, Greek, Roman, and Egyptian. Thus the symbols in the cards appear universal.

The cards date to a time when people were much closer to nature than we are today. Their surroundings, the sun, the stars, the forests, wild and domesticated animals were a source of protection and knowledge that helped them to survive. In present-day urban society we have lost touch with nature and our primitive instincts. Yet as the world becomes more populated and polluted, we are realizing that we cannot ignore nature. We are not a separate entity, but a vital part of the earth. The pictures on the cards are symbols of natural forces that we can relearn to use to our advantage. While the cards are useful in solving personal problems, they also always guide us to a common good.

The Cultural Tradition of Gypsy Fortune Telling

Gypsies in Russia have always been renowned for their fortune-telling abilities. This is due to their chosen lifestyle; freedom of movement physically, emotionally, and spiritually. One of the best descriptions of them is found in the poem, "Gypsies," written by the nineteenth-century Russian poet, Alexander Sergeyevich Pushkin. He described their lively freedom, their clamorous wandering through Bessarabia and the steppes (present day SW USSR). They led a simple, quite poor, yet peaceful existence.

The plot of the poem reveals the essence of gypsy freedom. Aleko, a fugitive from civilization, is found by the young gypsy, Zemfira, who takes him as a lover and brings him into the gypsy camp. He is very happy living the free life of wandering over the steppes and performing with a tame bear in various villages. Zemfira asks him if he regrets leaving the civilized world; the large buildings, fancy clothes, feasts, and beautiful girls. Aleko answers:

Regret what? If only you knew,
If you could imagine
The lack of freedom in the suffocating cities!
There people in crowds, fenced in,
Cannot breath the morning breeze,
Nor the spring scent of the meadows;
They are ashamed of love, persecute ideas,
Sell their own freedom,
Bow their heads in front of idols
And beg for money and chains.
What did I throw away? The agitation of betrayals,
The sentence of prejudice,
The crowds senseless persecution
Or brilliant disgrace.

However, the idyllic happiness does not last. After two years and one child, Zemfira has found another youth to love. She sings Aleko a song to tell him of her new love:

Old husband, formidable husband,
Stab me, burn me:
I am steadfast: I fear
Neither the knife, nor fire.

I hate you,
Despise you;
Another I love,
Loving I die.

Following the song, she tells him he is free to be angry. Aleko turns to Zemfira's father, who relates to him his own love for Zemfira's mother, who likewise fell in love with another and left him after one year. However, the father looks at the situation philosophically, comparing a young woman's love to the wandering moon:

Look: under the distant firmament
Wanders the unrestricted moon;
Passing she pours her radiance
On all nature alike.
She peeps in any cloud,
Illuminating it magnificently—
And now—she has crossed to another one;
And that one too she will not visit for long.
Who will show her her place in the sky,
Saying: stop there!
Who will say to the heart of a young maid,
Love only one, do not change?

Aleko can't accept this rationalization, and when he catches Zemfira with her lover he murders both of them. The gypsies do not punish him, but they no longer want him in their camp. He was not born to their way of life because he wanted freedom of choice for himself but couldn't accept it in Zemfira.

The poem has been retold to illustrate the gypsies' freedom of thought and action, which made them good fortune tellers. Not being restricted by laws and rules of civilization, they could easily see through the shams of peoples' lives in cities and villages. People usually get into dilemmas when they are trying to please or follow someone else's ideas, rather than remain in touch with their own inner being. The gypsies, loving honesty more than anything, were able to strip away the falseness of peoples' actions and in this way help them in solving their problems, which is the ultimate goal of fortune telling.

The gypsies were always welcome into the villages and cities. Their colorful, gay caravans brought diversion and entertainment to the inhabitants. Along with songs, entertainment, and trading, fortune telling was the most sought after activity. Besides their ability to look at things as they really are and not be afraid to voice these things, they also had an uncanny ability to foretell the future. Zemfira, in the poem, knows that she will be killed, yet this does not deter her from following her heart. This ability to foretell their own and other peoples' futures made them desirable visitors wherever they went.

The gypsies used a variety of tools in their fortune telling; from crystal balls, tea leaves, palm reading, playing cards to the present set of cards. Being closer to nature than city folks, they had simplified the complexities of life into simple symbols as illustrated in the cards. Each picture symbolizes a major theme, for example, HEART = love, MOON = peace, STAR = destiny, etc.

The pictures on the cards are symbols that activate the intuitive part of our brains. Our brains have logical and intuitive capabilities. Society demands logical thought and action that produce an orderly environment, and yet, at the same time, stifle the soul. Through the cards, the gypsies could unlock the intuitive side of peoples' natures. Not only could the gypsies interpret the cards, but the person having the reading done would intuitively know what the card was referring to. He or she could internally process the information or could discuss it with the gypsy or with friends to further clarify the meaning. Whether the person followed the advice or not was up to the individual. However, having released the intuitive side of his or her nature, a happy, carefree atmosphere prevailed and everyone enjoyed themselves.

Because gypsies loved freedom so passionately, they were persecuted by despotic leaders such as the Tsar, the Nazis, and later by Stalin. Their former lifestyle of wandering has been curtailed and many of their traditions have been lost. However, some gypsies can still be found in the USSR today. Most of them are prospering under the present administration. Their main activity is still fortune telling, although some have added the selling of miracle creams and cosmetics to their repertoire. People continue to want good fortune and miracles which the gypsies are happy to provide.

My Family History

My family's interest in Gypsies and fortune telling began with my mother's mother, Nadezhda Alexeyevna. From earliest childhood, she was fascinated with the Gypsies that came to her *datcha* (country home). She would sneak out at night to go to their camp and listen to the lively music and mesmerizing stories.

Following the Russian Revolution of 1917, she fled with my grandfather from Russia to Serbia. My grandfather, Victor Feadorovich Mashkov, had served previously as Russian consul to Serbia from 1898 to 1903.

Shortly after her arrival in Serbia, my grandmother became friends with a lively Gypsy, Milka. Milka was able to scrounge up all kinds of items that my grandmother needed to settle down. They developed a strong friendship in spite of the differences in class. They were a strange duo, one an intellectual, the other a child of nature. Milka never ceased to amaze my grandmother. Although they were good friends, Milka would nevertheless steal small objects from my grandmother by hiding them under her voluptuous breasts, and later give them as presents to others. Being discovered never stopped her, because embarrassment was not part of her psyche. In the same way, she would talk to anyone, from the Yugoslavian leader Tito to the poorest beggar. A common interest that bonded the two women was their interest in fortune telling. My grandmother was interested in using the Gypsy methods, although she had psychic abilities herself.

The 1920s and 1930s were an era when people were interested in mysticism, spiritualism, and the occult. Together, my grandparents were active in holding séances with other Russian aristocrats. My grandmother was also adept at card reading. My first acquaintance with the cards was watching my grandmother do readings during World War II. My grandmother was able to predict danger, and we survived the war without any casualties in our family.

Fate intervened and my family was displaced once more following World War II. We ended up in a Displaced Persons Camp. Everyone's concern was which country they should emigrate to. News spread that an eighty-year-old Russian woman was telling fortunes and advising people. My mother sought her out and was happy to discover that the woman was using cards similar to those her mother had used. The old woman valued my mother's interest in the cards and gave her the notes on how to read the cards. The old woman wanted the knowledge to be passed on to future generations, and not to disappear with her death. She said little about the origin of the cards, other than that they came from the Gypsies. She had brought them out of Russia following the Russian Revolution.

The cards were instrumental in my mother choosing to emigrate to Canada. There were other options such as Romania, Bulgaria, or Australia, but the cards were always negative for those choices. Coming to Canada, which the cards predicted would be successful, proved to be the best move that our family could have made.

On arrival in Canada, my mother painted the first set of cards based on the ones the old Russian woman had used. She used them for herself and her friends. When I came of age, I also wanted the cards. A second set was painted by my mother at that time for my use. Since then, both of us have used the cards extensively. As more and more friends and acquaintances wanted to have their cards read, I realized that I should translate the original Russian version. Once translated, the cards became even more popular. The constant requests to purchase a set of cards led me to write this book. With the publication of the cards and the book, I hope that the Gypsy tradition of fortune telling will be enjoyed and appreciated once again by everyone.

My own life has been enriched by the cards. From my late teenage days until the present, I have constantly used the cards. They have warned me of a tumor that was growing in my spine and could have left me paralyzed. Later, they helped me survive turbulence in my marriage, and guided me in making wise decisions about raising two sons. Likewise, they have helped me meet the challenges of the working world by warning me of danger, or telling me when to proceed at full force. Today, I am still happily married and have two successful sons. I have attained almost every goal that I have set out to achieve due to the cards. Every time I had a problem, the cards were my best friend. They helped me see the bright side even in the bleakest times, and encouraged me to take positive action.

The cards have also been a great source of entertainment. I have gone to many parties dressed as a gypsy and told fortunes. My friends and their friends have been coming to me for years to have their fortunes read. Most recently, since I finished the manuscript, people from all walks of life have been asking me to do a reading. On Halloween, I was invited by a group of university professors to do readings. At work, secretaries, janitors, cafeteria staff, cooks, and fellow teachers have been clamoring to have readings done. As the world gets more complicated and people face more decisions, the cards offer the reassurance and advice that people are seeking.

Because the cards have been such a positive influence in my mother's and my life, we see them as an enlightening force that can be beneficial to others who use them.

Translating the Cards

The major decision I had to make in translating the cards was whether to translate them word for word from the Russian or use the equivalent English expression, saying, or proverb. Although both the English and Russian languages belong to the Indo-European language group, the use and meanings of words have been influenced by different forces. The Russian language and thinking was influenced greatly by the Eastern cultures of China, India, and Turkey. Thus the Russian language and thought are more mystical. Mysticism is the doctrine that it is possible to achieve communion with God through contemplation and love without the medium of human reason. The West, on the other hand, has extolled the rational mind. Thus the dilemma: how do you translate that which is mystical into that which is rational?

My final decision was to translate as close to the Russian meaning as possible, even though it might sound grammatically strange in English. I felt that by giving the true Russian meaning, I would help the reader of the cards gain more of an understanding of the original meaning than if only the English equivalent was given. The English equivalents such as proverbs, colloquial expressions, and sayings are included in the paragraphs following the literal translation. These more detailed explanations are for the purpose of giving the parallel meaning in English and further explaining the various connotations of the card.

How to
Do A
Reading

1. Find a flat surface, at least 20 by 20 inches (51 by 51 cm). This can be a table, bed, floor, or the like.

2. Take the cards in your right hand, face up, and shuffle them into your left hand, toward your heart. Do this five to ten times to clear the deck.

3. *Concentrate* on what you want the cards to tell you. Either ask a question or go over the areas you want information on, such as love, money, health, success at a project, travel, what the future will bring. As you are concentrating, shuffle the cards again from right hand to left seven times. Have someone count the number of shuffles, or do it yourself. Stop after the seventh shuffle and hold the cards in your left hand without moving them about any further.

4. With your right hand, pick up the deck and place the cards on the table face down. With your left hand, cut the cards once toward you.

5. Once again pick up the cards with your right hand and place the deck in the palm of your left hand. Make sure you don't turn the cards any further as it can affect the reading of the last card.

6. Using your right hand, start laying the cards out. Take the top card and, turning it over, place it on the table right side up. Repeat with four more cards, placing each to the right of the last card.

7. You will have a row of five cards. See if any two adjoining cards will form a complete picture if rotated. (See figure 1.) Rotate these

cards to form the picture and push all five cards toward each other so they are touching.

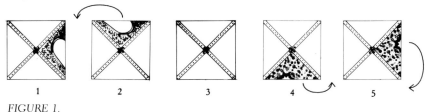

FIGURE 1.

8. Starting on the left again, lay five more cards under the first row. (See figure 2.) You can now turn each card in any direction to form a picture. However, don't switch places of cards. They can only be rotated in place. Continue laying the cards out until you have five rows of five cards each. Pay particular attention to the last card, not moving it unless a picture matches another card.

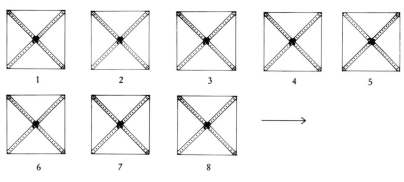

FIGURE 2.

I usually lay the cards out slowly, one card at a time, and try to find the matching pictures as I go along. Then at the end, I double check by looking for my favorite pictures or the pictures that would answer my question. Any pictures missed are usually spotted at this time.

9. Starting with the first row, if you have a matching picture, turn to the book and read the meaning for the picture. The picture can lie in any one of four positions:

Position 1—The arrow by the number on the picture points downward toward you.

Position 2—The arrow by the number points to the right.

Position 3—The arrow by the number points to the left.

Position 4—The arrow by the number points upward, away from you.

Read the meaning for the position in which the picture lies. Also read the general meaning of the picture and the more detailed information for the position it is in.

10. Continue reading the meaning for each picture that comes up as you go from the top left of the layout to the bottom right. If a card forms a picture in one position, and would form another picture with another adjoining card if you rotated it, then do readings for both pictures. Do the first one, then move the card so that you can get the second picture.

11. The last card you laid down is very important as it generally consolidates the meanings for the entire reading. Read the meanings for all four pictures represented on the card, whether or not any of the pictures is completed by an adjoining card. If a picture is completed by an adjoining card, read it first. Then proceed to read the meaning for the uncompleted pictures. For each picture read the meaning for the position it lies in. This shows you what the situation is right now. Then read the meaning for the picture in position 1. This shows you what the outcome of the situation will be. You may prefer to read only the meaning for position 1.

Most of the outcomes will be positive; however, a few pictures such as the HEARSE, MOUNTAINS, SCYTHE, and SNAKE warn you of danger when they are in position 1. Should you get one of these pictures on your last card, then you know that they forewarn you of serious danger. Examine negative things that you are doing in your life and try to change them. Remember, you are the pilot of your life; your action or inaction will determine what happens to you.

When reading this last card, read first the picture that has the most negative message. Save the picture with the most positive message for the end. It is always best to end on a positive note.

SPECIAL NOTE: If you are left-handed, then lay the cards out the way they are comfortable and natural to you. You can follow the preceding steps, but use the hand that is most comfortable.

Doing A Reading For Another Person

1. Shuffle the deck five to ten times to clear it.

2. Give the cards to the person for whom you are doing the reading. Ask her or him to shuffle the cards seven times, from right hand to left hand, while concentrating on a question or asking for a general reading, count the shuffles and tell the person when to stop. Ask her or him to place the cards on the table and cut with the left hand toward the heart.

3. Carefully pick up the deck and turn it upside down if the person is sitting across from you. Lay the cards out the same as for yourself.

4. Read the meaning for the position of the picture as it faces you, not the person you are doing the reading for. (If you had not turned the cards upside down, they would be facing the person you are doing the reading for. By turning the cards upside down, you make it easier for yourself to read the cards.)

5. Read the meaning for each picture that appears. Don't forget to read the meaning for each picture on the last card.

6. Explain that if popular pictures such as the MONEY, RING, SHIP, or others do not show up, it simply means that they are not important aspects in the person's life at this moment. In the same way, if the person is worried about her or his health and the HEARSE or FIREWOOD pictures don't show up, then there should be no concerns about the person's health at this time.

Doing A Reading For A Person Who Is Absent

1. Clear the deck.
2. Concentrate on the question(s) you want the deck to answer for the person you are doing the reading for.
3. Shuffle the cards seven times yourself.
4. Cut the deck once toward you.
5. Proceed to lay out the cards and read as if for yourself. You need not have the person's permission because you are doing the reading for your own information not for anyone else's. For example, you might want to know how your son or daughter who lives far away is doing but don't want to disturb him or her. By doing a reading you can settle your concerns.

Outcomes

WHAT SHOULD YOU DO IF FEW PICTURES COME UP?
Sometimes very few pictures come up for a reading. It can mean that the person did not concentrate very much while shuffling, due to too many distractions. Or it may be that the person is in the doldrums, a period when not much is happening in his or her life. In either case, *I would not redo the reading that day.*

If few pictures have come up, then you can do a *negative reading*—that is, a reading of what is *not* in store in the near future. For example, if the HEARSE, FIREWOOD, or CASTLE pictures didn't come up, then you can assume that the health of the person is satisfactory as there are no warnings. Likewise, if the MONEY pictures didn't show up, that means that there will be no change in the person's financial position in the near future. If the SHIP, ROAD, or BOY pictures didn't show up, it does not mean that the person will not go on a trip that he or she has already purchased tickets for, only that this may not be the best time to get full enjoyment from the adventure. The pictures that don't appear represent things that are not very important in the person's life at this point.

WHAT IF NEGATIVE PICTURES COME UP? When negative pictures come up for the person, don't skip over them. Read the picture as it lies and explain the seriousness of the situation, but *never* give fatalistic advice. People can have serious illnesses from which they can recuperate. Couples break up and then may reunite. The weather forecaster can give warnings of a hurricane approaching but does not tell you that you will die in it. In the same way, the cards warn people of danger, but each individual has his or her own way of facing the situation.

The person may reveal to you what the pictures refer to or may prefer to keep it private. The wonderful power of the cards is that they do promote talking about problems that may have been hidden and eating away at the person. On the other hand, sometimes even your best friends will have secrets that they will not divulge, no matter what. As a reader, *do not probe* into the problems of the people you read for; only give them the advice that the cards offer.

CAUTION: The cards are a game, intended for pleasure only. What is revealed is not intended to be relied upon. Individuals with problems should seek appropriate professional advice.

When To Do
A Reading

- A reading can be done anytime, anywhere.

- Do a reading only once a day per person, as you are getting the general flow of energy. Doing more than one reading in the same day interferes with this flow of energy and tampers with the advice.

- A reading can be done when you want a general forecast of the psychic energy around you, like a weather forecast. This can be done for yourself, for a group of friends who are with you, or even for someone who is close to you but not present at the time of the reading.

- The cards can be read when you have a problem that you want advice on. You can ask the cards a question you need guidance in resolving. The cards will not solve the problem for you, but will set out the situation, like a road map, so that all aspects will be revealed to you and you can chart the correct course. The cards are sometimes like the oracle at Delphi, speaking in riddles that you have to interpret.

- The cards can be read when you doubt someone's faithfulness. The cards will reveal if you have just cause to be suspicious or if you are simply being jealous.

- The cards can be read before taking a major trip to see if it will be free of worries or if unforeseen dangers lie ahead. For people who worry needlessly, the reading may eliminate unnecessary anxiety. Should there be a warning of danger, then extra precautions should be taken to avoid problems.

- The cards can be read when you are beginning a new venture. The cards will tell you the outcome of the venture or warn you of any complications or obstructions you may encounter on the way.

- The cards can be read when you are in a neutral zone, when nothing interesting is happening. The cards will either tell you that you should be happy where you are or will advise you of future unforeseen events.

- Traditionally, Friday was a good day to do a reading. People did not eat meat or dairy products on that day. This cleansed their bodies so they were more receptive to psychic vibrations. The cards were *never read on Sundays*. Sunday is a day of rest and going to church. A reading done on Sundays can be false.

- You may want to do a *forecast for the year*. On New Year's Day, a reading can be done that will predict the major events or experiences for the coming year. Formulate questions about what you would like to accomplish during the year, and the cards will reveal the outcome. Also, unthought-of events may be indicated. If only a few unimportant cards come up, don't despair, as it means it will be a relatively calm year, a year to gather thoughts and energies for future endeavors. I usually write down the predictions and refer to them several times during the year to see if they are coming true and if I am on track, flowing with the natural energy.

21

- In prerevolutionary Russia, various types of fortune telling were done on the eve of Christ's christening day, which falls twelve days after the birth of Christ. The Russian calendar was changed after the revolution to coincide with the Western one. According to the old Gregorian calendar, Christ was born on January 7, and his christening was on January 19. Therefore, on January 18 I usually have an evening with friends who are interested in fortune telling. I do my cards, while another friend does tarot cards and another does psychometry. It is a good idea to limit the group to no more than four people. If you have more, not everyone will have a chance to have a reading done, and you lose some of the intimate conversation that the cards encourage. The reading done will be for the year to come and even into the future. Again, write it down and look it over during the year.

Do's and Don'ts For Readings

- Don't charge money for doing a reading. Friends may bring wine or food as friendly gestures, but charging for the reading is not right.

- Do only one reading per person in one day.

- Don't do readings on Sundays.

- Don't do readings for children. Children can play with the cards, putting pictures together. There is nothing to harm the children; in fact, it is educational for them to match the pictures. However, the lives and brains of children are changing and expanding so rapidly that any prediction becomes obsolete almost instantaneously. Generally, cards can be read for someone over sixteen years of age, but again, events can happen too quickly at times to be predicted. Eighteen onward is a good age for doing readings.

- Do not use the cards to determine timing for criminal activity. It is acceptable to do a reading to see if you are financially lucky at a particular time and to follow by buying lottery tickets or even playing bingo or betting on horses. The cards do not guarantee winnings, they only tell you when the climate is fortunate. However, should you try to plan criminal activity, the cards will not give you a reliable answer.

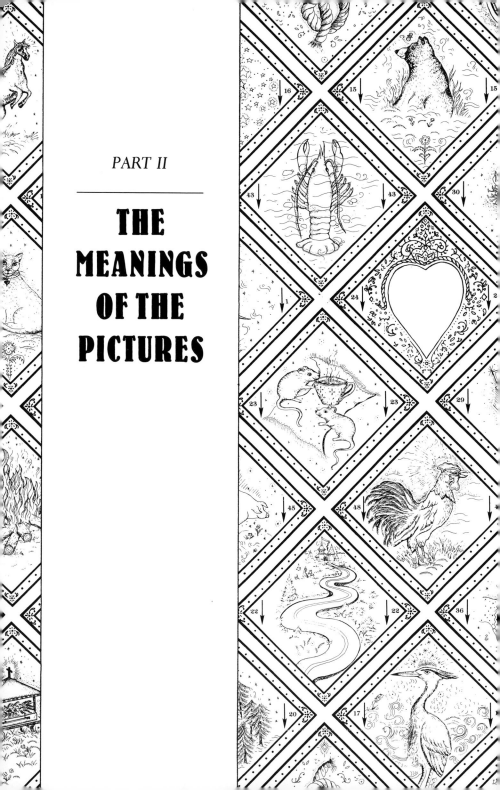

PART II

THE
MEANINGS
OF THE
PICTURES

HOW TO
UNDERSTAND THE
DESCRIPTION OF
EACH PICTURE

PERIOD OF INFLUENCE: The reading that you are doing may refer to events one to two weeks prior to the reading itself, or it may apply to present or future occurrences. Each picture has a different period of influence, indicated by one or more of the following words:

> **immediate**—refers to events one to two weeks prior to the reading, during the reading itself, or one to two weeks following the reading
>
> **short**— refers to events one to four weeks following the reading
>
> **middle**— refers to events one to several months following the reading
>
> **life**— indicates a lifelong effect

SYMBOL FOR: This is a very brief description of what the picture refers to. The actual meaning depends on the position of the picture.

MEANING: This is the English translation of the original Russian interpretation. The numbers 1, 2, 3, and 4 refer to the position of the picture—whether the arrow by the number on the picture points downward (position 1), right (position 2), left (position 3), or upward (position 4).

GENERAL MEANING OF PICTURE: This gives the background explanation for each picture. It explains the symbolism; why the picture represents what it does. There are symbols drawn from Egyptian times, Greek mythology, Christianity, medieval times, and the Russian countryside. Some symbols appear universal, while others are typical of Russian folklore. Having read this section once, you do not need to read it each time you do a card reading.

POSITIONS 1, 2, 3, and 4: These are more detailed explanations of the advice given by each picture, based on its position. English proverbs or colloquial expressions are used in this section. Some examples from readings I've done are included; they may not refer to your particular situation, but show possible interpretations depending on context. In addition, many Russian proverbs have been included to further show us reality in a different manner from what we are accustomed to seeing.

Generally, in positions 1 and 2 the pictures are positive, announcing good news. The picture in position 1 is the most positive and has the strongest meaning. In positions 3 and 4 the pictures are negative, warning you of danger.

position 1—strongest meaning
position 2—weaker
position 3—slightly negative
position 4—negative

However, a few of the pictures, such as the MOUNTAINS, HEARSE, SCYTHE, and DAGGER, are always negative. For these pictures, the negative warning is strongest in position 1 and weakest in position 4.

1 CAVALIER

PERIOD OF INFLUENCE: immediate to short

SYMBOL FOR: news

MEANING: ↓ 1. You will hear pleasant news.
         → 2. Unexpected happy news.
         ← 3. News that will bring a disappointment.
         ↑ 4. Unpleasant news.

GENERAL MEANING OF PICTURE: The cavalier was a gallant gentleman most often seen serving the king or helping ladies. He was a carrier of news before the coming of the post office. The news was generally of an important nature; however, the news could be frivolous or gossipy when dealing with women.

The cavalier today would be a bureaucrat, a lawyer, or someone working in middle management—someone who has the power of controlling information. Thus the news you will be receiving will be of an official type, or gossip relating to the inside information the cavalier has. Usually it will be oral communication.

The picture can indicate the answer to questions that you have asked. For example, if you have applied for a job, the picture can tell you if you will hear a positive or a negative response. However, it only refers to the initial news, not to the outcome of the situation. You may hear that you have been placed on a waiting list, which might be disappointing news to you, yet the outcome might be positive.

POSITION 1: You will hear pleasant news. If you have asked a question, then you know that you will hear a positive answer.

This is also a good time to seek advice or favors from those higher up than you, as they will be inclined to help you.

POSITION 2: Unexpected happy news. This is something you have not been consciously seeking, yet when the news arrives, it will make you very happy. You may hear your company is moving to a better location, or you may discover that the flu you thought you had is actually a long-awaited pregnancy. The news could also be of a gossipy nature, such as hearing that a politician you hate has been involved in a sex scandal. Generally, you will be privy to inside information, so that the news will excite you.

POSITION 3: News that will bring a disappointment. As mentioned earlier, the initial news will bring a disappointment, but this does not mean your plan has been defeated for all time. Perhaps you have been placed on a waiting list, or your proposal needs changes. If you are prepared by a reading before you hear the disappointing news, then the news will not shock you. You will be able to ask questions and obtain suggestions with a clear head, making you better prepared for the next round.

POSITION 4: Unpleasant news. If you have asked a question, then the answer will be a negative one. You can do little at the present time to change the circumstances.

2 CLOVER

PERIOD OF INFLUENCE: middle

SYMBOL FOR: luck

MEANING: ↓ 1. Happiness and fulfillment of desires.
        → 2. Happiness slightly clouded by a misunderstanding.
        ← 3. Sorrow for a short duration, which will have a satisfactory outcome.
        ↑ 4. Considerable grief or disappointment.

GENERAL MEANING OF PICTURE: The clover is a plant that enriches the soil; consequently, it has been associated with good pastures and good luck. Nature is going out of its way to enrich your life. You have little to do, other than enjoy the bountiful harvest.

The clover generally refers to one's immediate surroundings or environment. This includes your home, job, family, or recreational activities. It generally refers to one's emotional state rather than material surroundings. You are happy because good luck is smiling at you, rather than due to the details.

The ironic aspect of this picture is that sometimes we are happy without knowing it. The picture is a gentle reminder to count our blessings when the going is good.

POSITION 1: The clover brings happiness and fulfillment of desires. The picture tells you that luck is with you now. Good things will come your way by pure chance. If you have asked a question on the outcome of some matter, then you know that it will turn out well, making you happy. You might already be having the good luck. The picture covers events shortly preceding the reading, as well as present and near future happenings.

The clover picture is strong, and refers to fulfillment of important desires in your life. You could meet the man or woman of your dreams, get the job you have been dreaming of, or stop smoking for the final time.

POSITION 2: Happiness slightly clouded by a misunderstanding. Happiness is the ultimate good, but it can't be achieved by itself. We get it from having health, wealth, knowledge, friendship, and virtue. The achieving of any one of these leads to happiness, but if we pursue only one aspect, such as wealth, and not the others, then we cannot attain happiness. What are you doing that is preventing you from being totally happy? Are you devoting too much time to your work and neglecting your family? Are you forgetting to communicate with people around you? Are you obsessed with a problem that can be resolved by simply asking a question? Whatever misunderstanding exists, it should be fairly easy to solve, as the CLOVER picture brings luck to it.

POSITION 3: Sorrow for a short duration, which will have a satisfactory or happy outcome. Your luck is down right now, but it is only for a short duration. You could be out of a job, could have failed a test, or could have seen your best friend move to another part of the country. However, although you might not be happy at the time, a positive solution to the dilemma will develop. You will find a new job, pass the course, find a new way of communicating with your friend, and so forth. The secret is not to get too despondent over the situation. Think of it as a time out, a time to rethink your position and begin anew. You can increase your luck by socializing with people, listening to your hunches, examining the possibilities very carefully and then taking a chance, and believing in yourself. The CLOVER picture is on your side. Remember the Russian proverb: Without pain, there is no learning.

POSITION 4: Considerable grief or disappointment. The luck is not with you right now. Events may happen that you have little control over that will bring you grief. People die, companies collapse, governments change, but the world goes on. Take the time to mourn the grief or disappointment, so that you can put it to rest.

The grief or disappointment might be in regard to your own endeavors, or it can refer to someone who is very close to you. In either case you will be affected emotionally. Again a Russian proverb applies here: People plan, but God disposes.

3   SHIP

PERIOD OF INFLUENCE: middle

SYMBOL FOR: finances, adventure

MEANING: ↓ 1. You will receive an inheritance or a winning.
→ 2. Riches due to trade or labor.
← 3. Travel.
↑ 4. Material loss or unsuccessful efforts.

GENERAL MEANING OF PICTURE: The ship is closely related to one's money situation. It speaks of riches and adventure. In the early days of exploration, ships set forth to discover new lands and bring back riches. The ship is similar to number 5 in numerology, which stands for adventure, travel, and experience. The picture encourages action of some sort. Whenever the picture is in position 1, one can take financial chances that normally would not be recommended. However, if the picture is in position 4, it is a warning to be careful in money or business matters.

POSITION 1: You will receive an inheritance or a winning. In modern days this can refer to any unexpected source of money. This is an opportune time to buy lottery tickets, gamble, or take financial chances. It must be stressed that you are not going to win something every time the picture comes up, only that your chances of winning are greater during this time. Likewise, the money doesn't only come from your planned action but can come from any direction. An inheritance implies that the money can come from some forgotten source. Perhaps you have a relative you have forgotten about, or you have some old stocks or bonds that can be cashed in now for a profit.

This is a good time to close any deal that you began earlier. Commissions or bonuses may also be in store. A warning: the cards should not be used to make a profit in an illegal way.

POSITION 2: Riches due to trade or labor. The explorers set out for unknown lands and faced many adventures, with the result that some of them came back with cargoes worth a fortune. In the same way, if you make the effort, you can be rewarded with financial gain. This is a good time to sell things or make money due to your labor. If you are unemployed, then this is an excellent time to start a business of your own or apply for jobs. You will have excellent results as long as you make the effort. Apply the Russian proverb: Forge the iron while it is hot.

POSITION 3: Travel. This picture indicates that this is a favorable time to make a trip. Generally it refers to distant places, not just weekend jaunts. Should this picture come up in conjunction with the ROAD picture, then a trip is very likely. If you have already planned a trip and this picture comes up, it means that things will go smoothly during your travels and you will have a good time.

POSITION 4: Material loss or unsuccessful efforts. Not every explorer came back with riches. Christopher Columbus discovered North America yet did not bring back gold to make him rich. Thus not all your efforts will be successful. This is not a time to gamble or take financial chances. You should be careful in investment matters, perhaps not putting all your money into one venture in case the ship sinks with all the assets aboard. The Russian proverb states: Overseas there is a cow that costs half a penny. Although things may be cheap in other countries, they are expensive to bring back. Thus your ideas may be good but may not be practical financially.

4 HOUSE

PERIOD OF INFLUENCE: immediate to middle

SYMBOL FOR: household or business affairs

MEANING: ↓ 1. You will enjoy success in all affairs.
→ 2. The right step will bring you success.
← 3. Beware of the people surrounding you.
↑ 4. Failure in some newly planned project.

GENERAL MEANING OF PICTURE: The HOUSE, like the CLOVER picture, denotes good luck. The house or shelter is one of our primary concerns, secondary only to food and water. Having a well-constructed house enables one to pursue other business. The HOUSE picture refers to material well-being, the economic aspects of the house or family situation. The picture also can refer to job situation and business affairs as they have a direct bearing on the security of the family. It is a good picture to receive for someone who is concerned with the material outcome of a situation.

POSITION 1: This is a wonderful picture to get in this position. It affirms that everything in your house is going to be successful. Whether you live in a house, apartment, or anywhere else, the household will be secure and happy. Any project that you undertake, whether it be fixing your house or beginning a new job, will go smoothly and successfully. This picture can appear even amidst a bankruptcy, indicating that you will have as successful a settlement as is possible under the circumstances. If you are beginning a new endeavor and this picture comes up, then you should go full force because success is likely.

POSITION 2: The right step will bring you success. This is like the oracle of Delphi, speaking in riddles. How do you know what the right step is? This is a time to examine your options carefully and go with the one that seems correct to you. The answer is within you, you only need to learn to focus on the problem and listen to your own instincts for the answer. Usually the instinct only comes once and then our rational mind takes over and begins to rationalize or place the learned acceptable values on the situation. When the picture comes up for you in this position, go forth with your unique ideas, no matter how far out they may seem to the average observer. Remember that every new idea was at first met with suspicion and opposition.

POSITION 3: Beware of the people surrounding you. Someone could be doing something that can cause you an economic setback. It could be someone who is fixing your house and overcharging you for the work. Or perhaps someone at work is blocking your plans or taking credit for your work.

The picture can also refer to someone in your immediate household who is a danger to you now. It can be someone who is usually a good person, yet due to alcohol, drugs, or even medicine may become violent and cause you harm. This is not the time to provoke the person or try and resolve problems. The HOUSE picture is an immediate picture, meaning that the situation will not last long. Therefore, bide your time and wait to deal with problems until a more favorable time.

When this picture comes up, it is also a good idea to make sure you lock the doors to your house and take precautions against break-ins or burglaries. This is not the time to invite strangers to your house or to be too trustful of neighbors. Follow the Russian proverb: Depend on God, but don't be careless yourself.

POSITION 4: Failure in some newly planned project. This does not mean that the project is doomed for all time, only that at this moment it is unsuccessful. Perhaps you want to paint the steps to your house, but you find that all kinds of other things come up and you don't have time to do it.

The picture can also refer to projects at work. You have submitted your plans and they come back rejected. It does not mean that you should abandon the idea, only that you will have to make some revisions before it is accepted. If you do a reading on the success or failure of a project and the HOUSE picture comes up in this position, then you are forewarned and the actual rejection won't be such a shock. You will be in a better frame of mind to listen to the suggestions that are offered to improve the project.

5 FIREWOOD

PERIOD OF INFLUENCE: immediate

SYMBOL FOR: physical health

MEANING: ↓ 1. A good state of health.
 → 2. Recovery.
 ← 3. A minor illness.
 ↑ 4. A bruise, cut, or illness.

GENERAL MEANING OF PICTURE: Firewood is used to keep us warm and healthy when the weather is cold. This picture refers to the immediate condition of our physical health. Those who are hypochondriacs, seeing the doctor at every sign of illness, should rest assured that this picture does not refer to life-and-death types of illness. The HEARSE picture refers to more serious illnesses.

POSITION 1: A good state of health. If you are worried about your health, then you can stop worrying. Everything you are doing is contributing to your physical well-being. Sometimes people get this picture when they are involved in some kind of problem. The picture comes up in this position to assure them that whatever worry they have, it is not affecting their health. When older people get this picture, it can be very reassuring to them. Even though they are slowing down and not as full of vim and vigor as they used to be, nevertheless they are healthy.

POSITION 2: Recovery. Whatever illness you have had, you will recover. The illness could have been a cold, a flu, or something more serious. Whatever medicine or methods you have been using to cure yourself are working and you should continue them until you have fully recovered. To those people who have had minor pains and aches but no major illness, this picture can be reassuring. Their aches were not imaginary. The picture signals an end to those discomforts and good health to follow.

POSITION 3: A minor illness. This could be a cold, a flu, or an irritation of some kind. It is not a major illness, as the HEARSE picture would indicate that. If you are not sick when you get this picture, then it might be a good idea to watch your diet, get adequate rest, and not do any activity that might influence your health negatively. When your Russian friends greet you in the morning with, "You look like you have been carrying water for the devil the whole night," you know that you are overextending yourself.

If you do get ill, it will not last long. Usually it will go away by itself and you won't even have to consult a doctor about it. However, make sure you do get adequate rest and a healthy diet so that it doesn't escalate into something more serious.

POSITION 4: A bruise, cut, or illness. You might already have hurt yourself in some way or are about to do it. We usually hurt ourselves when we are rushing around, not paying attention to what we are doing. It might be a good idea to slow down and be more careful. If you are planning to drink, then don't drive a car. Don't do any foolish things at this time as injury will result. The Russian proverb states: If you knew where you'd fall, you'd place some straw there. In this case you know that an injury may happen; therefore, be careful. In any case, the injury or illness will not be major and will go away soon.

6 APPLE

PERIOD OF INFLUENCE: immediate

SYMBOL FOR: encounter

MEANING: ↓ 1. A pleasant happening.
  → 2. A pleasant unexpected occurrence, a present.
  ← 3. An unpleasant meeting, encounter.
  ↑ 4. An unpleasant occurrence in the near future.

GENERAL MEANING OF PICTURE: Like the student bringing an apple to the teacher to make him or her happy, the apple refers to little things that make us happy or cause us irritation. This is not a major card in our life, yet it is important in determining our attitude toward daily occurrences. If we can learn to enjoy pleasant happenings and tolerate unpleasant ones, then we can lower our stress level and enjoy life more. Remember, an apple a day keeps the doctor away.

POSITION 1: A pleasant happening. This could be a party, a luncheon, or even just having coffee with people who make you feel comfortable or happy. If you have been in the doldrums, then you should do some activity that gives you pleasure. Go to the movies, to a football game, to a play or a concert. In the same way that people enjoy eating an apple, do something sensuous to make you happy.

POSITION 2: A pleasant unexpected occurrence, a present. This refers to the unexpected occurrences that make life so interesting. Perhaps you will run into a friend you haven't seen for a long time, or you will get the theater tickets you have been trying to get. The present you get doesn't have to be gift-wrapped, rather it can be a child's first attempt at a Mother's Day or Father's Day card. Whatever pleasant occurrence happens, enjoy it—it's meant to brighten your life. The Russians say: It is better to have a small fish than a big cockroach. In other words, it's better to be happy with something small than unhappy with a big unpleasantness.

POSITION 3: An unpleasant meeting, encounter. This could be an unpleasant conversation or lack of one with a sales clerk, a run-in with your neighbor, or an upsetting meeting with your former lover. Sometimes people are so absorbed in their own problems or so genuinely busy that they present an abrasive side of their nature. Any encounter with them is unpleasant and may make our blood pressure go up. This is a wrong reaction. We should acknowledge that the problem is with the other person and not let his or her bad attitude affect us. It only takes one bad apple to spoil a whole barrel. Therefore, detach yourself from the bad apple—give him or her a big smile and proceed with your business. Follow the Russian proverb: Don't listen with your ears, but with your feet. In other words, if you don't like what is being said, leave.

POSITION 4: An unpleasant occurrence in the near future. This can refer to an actual argument with a sales clerk, neighbor, or former lover. The unpleasant occurrence is of a minor type and should not be allowed to spoil your day. If you can apply reason rather than emotion to the situation, you can negate the unpleasantness. The Russians kid: The farther you go into the forest, the more wood you will pile up. The proverb also applies to entering into disagreements. The more you argue, the more hurt piles up. At this time, don't add to the unpleasantness by being a boor yourself. Let the other person enjoy the role alone.

Recently the APPLE picture came up for me in position 4. I wondered what might happen, thinking it could be something serious, and I was on guard. Two days later my friend and I went for a psychic reading to a place quite far from my house. Only fifteen numbers were given out for turns at the reading, and in the shuffle we ended up having the last two numbers. My friend kept her number but I gave mine to a man who had come before me but ended up without one because someone else had pushed in and grabbed a number out of turn. I could have been upset, but I felt that this was one of life's little irritations that was not worth getting upset about. We had a lovely lunch, my friend had a good reading, and I will go back another time.

7 SNAKE

PERIOD OF INFLUENCE: immediate to middle

SYMBOL FOR: attack by someone

MEANING: ↓ 1. A verbal sting by a malicious person.
→ 2. Betrayal, unfaithfulness.
← 3. Loss.
↑ 4. Bitter jealousy.

GENERAL MEANING OF PICTURE: The snake is a strongly negative picture that warns you of evil forces. It is like the serpent in the Garden of Eden that tempted Eve to eat the forbidden fruit. Generally it means some force outside of us influencing our life in a negative way.

However, the snake may also be seen in a positive light. Venom is used in medicine to cure people. The serpent may be seen as the giver of life: it was only after Adam and Eve ate the apple given by the serpent that life began as we know it today. Just as the snake sheds its skin when it outgrows it, so the snake symbolizes our giving up one type of life for another. This may be the result of getting more knowledge than we want, which forces us to change our values.

POSITION 1: A verbal sting by a malicious person. Like the bite of a snake, it is usually unexpected and undeserved. The person isn't necessarily evil; rather, you have come in contact with the person when he or she is in a bad mood. The person is venting his or her frustrations on you. The remark stings because it touches a weak spot in you—your Achilles' heel. Other pictures in the deck will tell you how to react to the sting. The sting will smart for a while, but it will

44

go away. Perhaps the experience will show you your weak spot and you will do something to improve it. The sting may act like the venom that cures certain illnesses.

You can try to avoid a sting or minimize its bite by being circumspect in all your actions and avoiding confrontations.

POSITION 2: Betrayal, unfaithfulness, treachery, treason. If you are doing a reading to find out if someone is being unfaithful and the picture comes up in this position, then you can be sure that it is happening. The picture may also be a warning to those who don't suspect anything. Conversely, if you suspect unfaithfulness and the picture doesn't come up, then your suspicions are wrong. Over the years, I've found the picture to be quite accurate in revealing adulterous behavior. However, the picture is ambiguous in that it does not say which partner is being unfaithful. Only the person for whom the reading is being done knows which partner is being unfaithful.

If the picture does not refer to a sexual betrayal, then it could refer to anyone around you. There is a serpent in your environs who is leading you astray. It may be someone you don't even suspect. The Russian proverb warns: In deep, still pools of water, devils breed. A person may appear quiet and pleasant but inside be seething with anger, jealousy, or desire. Be on the lookout for a betrayal. Read all documents carefully before signing, avoid taking chances with the law, and don't leave yourself vulnerable to being deceived.

POSITION 3: Loss. This may be the loss of a person's affection for you or the loss of values that have been important to you. Just as the snake sheds its skin, so we are prone to changes in our lives. The changes may be good or bad, depending on how you view them. Loss of innocence is always painful, yet it is necessary if you are ever to attain wisdom. Young people might find it unimaginable that someone could forgive adulterous behavior in a partner. Yet the knowledge that a partner is unfaithful should lead one to examine one's own behavior. What actions or lack thereof on your part led the other person to stray? Thus the loss may lead to a growth in your understanding of yourself, your values, and your goals in life. Remember: To live a lifetime isn't like crossing a field. One will find many obstacles in a lifetime; some will be minor like hills, while others will be major like mountains. It is only when we learn to deal with our obstacles or problems that true growth and contentment can be achieved.

The loss may also be of something that you value very highly, like loss of a material possession or loss of reputation. As mentioned earlier, be very careful and circumspect when the SNAKE picture appears.

POSITION 4: Bitter jealousy. This may be your own feeling or someone else's. Either way, the emotion is not a healthy one. Jealousy is called the green-eyed monster because of the destruction it can cause. It distorts the vision of the person who is jealous, making him or her miss opportunities for making good friendships or enduring relationships. In a love situation, jealousy doesn't show how much you love the other person, but how insecure you are.

The cards have always been a help to people in revealing whether a partner is faithful or not. When their suspicions are alleviated, they don't need to waste energy on jealous feelings.

Should the picture refer to someone else's being jealous of you, try to defuse the jealousy. Flaunting your good fortune in front of others is never a good idea. Be honest and appreciative of the other person's good qualities. Once people realize that we are all in the same boat, jealousy may disappear.

8 HEARSE

PERIOD OF INFLUENCE: immediate to middle

SYMBOL FOR: danger to physical and emotional state

MEANING: ↓ 1. Sickness.
      → 2. A loss of condition, although only temporarily.
      ← 3. An unquestionable unpleasantness to which you will be subjected or fall prey.
      ↑ 4. You will escape danger in time.

GENERAL MEANING OF PICTURE: The picture at first appears frightening because it indicates death. However, *it does not mean that death is imminent*, it only warns us of the possibility. The FIREWOOD picture also deals with health problems, but of a more minor nature. When you get the HEARSE picture, you know that the problem is serious and not to be avoided.

Unlike the other pictures, which are usually positive in position 1 and get progressively more negative, the hearse is strongest in the position 1 and weaker in position 4.

If the picture appears completed on the last card in your layout, read only the meaning for the position in which it appears, not for position 1.

POSITION 1: Sickness. The sickness may lead to death if it is not attended to. In the introduction to the book, I have written about my experience of getting the picture. The picture warned me of a tumor that was growing in my spine. When you get this picture, you should reexamine your health. If anything is wrong, no matter how slight, you should see a doctor about it. Even if the doctor doesn't find anything wrong, you should start taking better care of your health. Perhaps you should be getting more rest, eating a better diet, exercising more, quitting your drinking to excess or smoking, or simply drinking more water. Many illnesses, such as heart trouble, cancer, diabetes, arthritis, and ulcers, take time to develop into serious conditions. The picture warns you that something you are doing is wrong and may result in a serious illness.

If you already have a serious illness and the picture keeps appearing for you, it means that you should continue using the medication or treatment prescribed. A friend who had cancer still had the picture appear following surgery. It did not mean that she was not cured, which she was. The picture warned her that the lifestyle that led to the cancer had to be abandoned forever. The new lifestyle—a better diet, more rest and exercise—had to be continued if good health was to last. The picture will disappear once you begin to take better care of your health.

POSITION 2: A loss of condition or state, although only temporarily. This is a feeling of total helplessness, not knowing what to do. An emotional upheaval has left you temporarily unstable, off balance. The emotional upheaval may have been brought about by a death in the family, loss of a job, finding out your spouse is unfaithful, children rebelling, or not knowing what to do next in your life.

The positive aspect of the card is that it tells you this is a temporary state. When you look at the situation carefully, you will realize that it is not of your doing. You can't change it but can only endure it. All of us have difficult situations thrust upon us at some times in our lives. If you can regard the situation as temporary, you can live through it with a minimum of damage to your health and emotional well-being.

POSITION 3: An unquestionable unpleasantness to which you will be subjected or fall prey. Something unpleasant is in store for you. It could be a loss of a job, being forced to move, family arguments, or unpleasant news of some kind. The situation is taxing your health, leaving you stressed.

This picture appeared for a friend before he lost his job. It was an unpleasant time for him but nothing he could do anything about as the seeds of the situation had been sewn a long time prior to the firing. Looking back at it four years later, he realized it was the best thing that could have happened to him. It was the end of one period in his life and the beginning of a new period.

POSITION 4: You will escape danger in time. In position 4, the picture is least threatening. Generally, you already know where in your life you are taking chances. The picture is a warning that at this particular time you should avoid all risks. If you are smoking or drinking too much, then it is time to stop or cut back. Are you driving a car that has faulty brakes? This is the time to check all aspects of your life. Don't take unnecessary chances emotionally or physically.

A friend had the picture appear for her when she was having a lot of problems economically and in her marriage. When warned of danger, she immediately acknowledged that her stomach was giving her trouble. Following the reading, she went to the doctor, who found that she had an ulcer developing. With proper diet, she was able to control it and avoid further serious problems.

9 BOUQUET

PERIOD OF INFLUENCE: immediate to short

SYMBOL FOR: happiness

MEANING: ↓ 1. Great success in all affairs.
  → 2. Winnings.
  ← 3. Fulfillment of a hope.
  ↑ 4. You will find a means of earning money.

GENERAL MEANING OF PICTURE: A bouquet of flowers is the reward that you get for spending many hours in the garden, planting, weeding, fertilizing, watering, and so forth. Thus this picture speaks of the final success that you achieve due to your efforts. It is not a free gift of nature, like the BIRDS or the CLOVER, but something that you have put an effort into earning.

POSITION 1: Good fortune in all pursuits. Great success awaits you in all your business affairs. If you asked a question of the reading and this picture comes up in this position, then you know the answer is positive. As mentioned in the general meaning, success is usually due to an earlier effort exerted by you. If you are beginning a project or halfway through and the picture comes up, then you know you are on the right path and are doing everything correctly. Just keep on working and success will be yours.

POSITION 2: Winnings, a monetary gain. This could mean an increase in salary, some new income from investments, or even winnings from a lottery ticket. However, the same as for the MONEY picture, it doesn't mean that you will receive money every time this

50

picture comes up, only that this is an opportune time to gain money. This would be a good time to ask for a raise, to evaluate your investment portfolio, or to buy a lottery ticket. As the Russians say: Under a stationary rock, water doesn't flow. A rock can symbolize stability, yet it can also stand for rigidity. Sometimes you have to let go, take a chance, in order to win. If you don't buy a lottery ticket, you can't win the prize.

POSITION 3: Fulfillment of a hope. The hopes people have vary from something as small as losing ten pounds to something as lofty as climbing Mt. Everest. In order to be fulfilled, your hope only needs to be something you want to do and are physically and mentally capable of doing. If this picture comes up, then your hope will turn to reality. Just remember that it takes long hours to become a champion in any field, so don't give up. Work toward your goal and you will achieve it. The Russians say: The hen only eats a grain at a time but eventually she gets full.

POSITION 4: You will find a means of earning money. The picture in this position is especially welcome to those who are unemployed, in fear of losing their jobs, or thinking about a career change. It means that if you examine your qualifications and look at your abilities, you will be able to find a means of earning money. The secret is to relax, examine the options, and be available to new opportunities. Many people become despondent when faced with unemployment and fail to realize that this can be an exciting opportunity for a new start.

Once I heard a person being interviewed on a radio show tell of an Indian chant that one is to repeat while meditating or throughout the day to help one find a means of earning a living. The chant is not to be used to improve one's job or make one rich, but rather to open the way for nature to provide for one's needs, the way nature provides seeds for birds when they are hungry. After chanting it, I received employment from most unusual places. For example, an elderly pensioner came from across town for a Russian lesson and insisted on paying me five dollars. This is the type of thing the BOUQUET picture in position 4 indicates will happen.

10   SCYTHE

PERIOD OF INFLUENCE: immediate to life

SYMBOL FOR: fate upsetting your life

MEANING: ↓ 1. Evil fate pursues you.
→ 2. You will hear a threat that will have consequences.
← 3. You will escape a catastrophe.
↑ 4. Quarrel.

GENERAL MEANING OF PICTURE: This picture refers to forces outside your control. Like the scythe that cuts long grass, a force is working on sabotaging your life. Those who are familiar with the theory of karma and reincarnation in Hinduism might interpret the picture as referring to misconduct in past lives that you are paying for in this life. For example, according to this theory, if you killed someone or were cruel in your past life, then in the next life you will have cruel things done to you. The picture can be interpreted from this viewpoint, or it can simply be interpreted from the viewpoint that in nature, bad things counterbalance good things; night follows day. During some parts of your life bad things will happen, and you should learn to accept them when they occur. The advantage of using the cards is that you can be warned of bad periods and have time to brace yourself.

The scythe being held by Father Time, a symbol we see on New Year's Eve, symbolizes the end of the old. When the scythe mows down the wheat, grass, or weeds, it clears the land for new growth. At the same time it clears your path of vision. A fresh start is possible.

POSITION 1: Evil fate pursues you. It is nothing that you can do anything about. All that you can do is accept it and live with it. This picture has come up for a friend of mine who is Jewish. She had to leave Poland partly because of being Jewish. At the time of the reading, she was still having problems because of her race. It was nothing that she could do anything about, only accept it and stop feeling persecuted. Another friend has this picture come up quite regularly. She had a bad childhood with an alcoholic parent. Again, she cannot change her past, but she can change her feelings toward the past. Once one is reconciled with what is, then this picture appears less often if at all.

The picture may also refer to an evil person who has entered your life. It may be a person at work, a student in your class, a neighbor, or a crank phone caller. You may unintentionally become the target of their outbursts. Try not to antagonize the person and seek help from legal sources.

POSITION 2: You will hear a threat that will have consequences. The picture warns you of the likelihood of a loss of some kind. It could be a loss of a job, a living space, or someone's affection. It is up to you to examine your circumstances to make sure you are not contributing to the problem. Remember, a scythe cuts down both wheat and weeds. You may get caught up in a company reshuffle and suffer as a result.

A friend had the picture appear just before he was fired unexpectedly. The company had to trim its staff, and my friend's manager, who was jealous of his abilities, took the opportunity to have him fired. However, my friend was partially to blame as his behavior had antagonized his superior. Had he been more careful, he perhaps could have prevented the situation.

POSITION 3: You will escape some catastrophe. Because you escape the catastrophe, you might not even be aware of its occurrence. Just be happy that trouble is avoiding you. However, when you do get this picture, make sure you listen to traffic reports, check weather conditions, and do everything you can to avoid being in a place or position where misfortune may happen.

The picture appeared in this position for a couple who were visiting from California. A week later there was an earthquake near their home, yet they were not hurt or affected in any way.

POSITION 4: Quarrel. This could be a quarrel in the family, with friends, associates, or at the work place. It is not something that you will start, but will be dragged into. Keep your wits about you, listen more than talk. In this way you can walk out of the situation with the least amount of damage to yourself or others. Remember, the scythe clears out a lot of the old, enabling a fresh start. In the same way, a quarrel can clear out a lot of old, repressed feelings and make possible a new start.

11 BRANCHES

PERIOD OF INFLUENCE: immediate to life

SYMBOL FOR: reconciliation or unpleasantness in
family relations

MEANING: ↓ 1. Making up after a quarrel.
           → 2. Disagreement in the family.
           ← 3. A breakup with a close person.
           ↑ 4. Tears, an offense.

GENERAL MEANING OF PICTURE: The branches refer to our
family structure or to people whom we consider our family. The tree
is the family while the branches are the individuals in the family. As
branches grow in different directions, so people within a family have
different interests and ideas. Sometimes the differences cause disagreements. Thus the picture deals with family unity or disunity.
Other than in position 3, it does not have long-term effects. Because
you see your family members more often than anyone else, you tend
to have more upheavals with them. Few people would vent their
frustrations at their boss, yet they do it at home all the time. The
picture refers to the many little arguments and unpleasantnesses that
occur in a family setting. More serious problems are indicated by the
HANDSHAKE and RING pictures.

POSITION 1: Making up after a petty quarrel or tiff. This is a
positive and welcome picture. It signifies an end to a quarrel or
misunderstanding. Usually the agreement comes of its own accord. A
sense of contentment accompanies the picture. A kiss or an embrace
will smooth over the matter. All bad feelings will be forgotten.

POSITION 2: Disagreement in the family. One family member wants something done one way while the other wants it done another way. The disagreement could have happened already or it could be about to happen. Sometimes this picture comes up when everything is going great in the family and there are no disagreements. Yet out of the blue, something comes up and you begin arguing. Even if you try to maintain your cool and not add to the quarrel, the other person will argue for both parties and a disagreement will ensue. The best advice is to accept the inevitable and wait it out. Usually after a week, the feelings that caused the disagreement will have passed and harmony is possible again.

POSITION 3: A breakup with a close person. In this position, the picture indicates disagreement of a serious nature. Some of the bitterest feuds can exist in families where members don't speak to each other for decades; yet the misunderstandings that caused the split are generally of a minor nature. Perhaps you weren't invited to a gathering, or notified of an event; you may feel neglected; or you may have suffered any of the many slights that occur in family life. Your immediate response is to retaliate by rejecting the other person.

A total breakup is possible at this time if both parties are entrenched in their views. You can't do much to change the other person's viewpoint, but you can reexamine your own contribution to the matter. See where you have made mistakes and try to correct your faults. Sometimes it's very difficult to see your faults, but remember there are always two armies in a war, otherwise there wouldn't be a conflict. By correcting your faults, you will find that a relationship that seems hopeless can be straightened out.

During a long marriage, the picture may appear many times. If the partners are willing to work on improving themselves, then the marriage will be restored.

The picture may also refer to a member of the family's moving far away from the home setting. This person has moved to a new area where he or she is beginning to set up new routes. The picture may appear to you as a reminder that you have to let go of the old feelings and ties.

POSITION 4: Tears, an offense. Unhappiness due to someone else's lack of consideration or hurtful actions. This is not a major problem in your life, just a period when you are feeling vulnerable. The other person might not even realize that he or she is hurting your feelings. If the tears come, cry as much as you can. This will wash away the negative feelings and leave you ready to face the world once again.

12   BIRDS

PERIOD OF INFLUENCE: immediate

SYMBOL FOR: freedom from responsibilities

MEANING: ↓ 1. Joy, merriment.
 → 2. Unexpected pleasure.
 ← 3. You expect someone not to fulfill a promise and you will be right.
 ↑ 4. An obstacle with which you will have to fight.

GENERAL MEANING OF PICTURE: Birds suggest freedom of flight; they have no worries or cares to hold them down. A bird is free to soar to heights that we cannot obtain by ourselves. It can fly and enjoy itself. It can look down from above at the world below it. For us it is just as important to let go and be like the bird, flying smoothly and easily in the air, landing only when we want to.

Birds are nature's friends. They signify freedom and unconstrained joy. They remind us of our free soul, unrestrained by the rules of our civilization. However, when the birds come in contact with civilization such as farms and airports, they become a nuisance to us. In the first two positions of this picture they represent joy and merriment, while in the last two, obstacles that we have to deal with.

POSITION 1: Joy, merriment, happiness, celebration, good times. The picture in this position refers to present circumstances or one of short duration. It could be an achievement, a promotion, a new job or apartment, or simply a reunion with good friends that makes you happy. As two birds are shown, it is a good time to spend with friends.

58

Any social activity will run smoothly with everyone having a good time. The point is, do something special so that good times will be remembered.

POSITION 2: Unexpected pleasure. Perhaps unexpected company will drop by, or you will decide at the last moment to do something and it will turn out well. Like the birds, we must learn to be carefree at times, to forget our obligations and simply have a good time. Stop doing the dishes and go to the movies with your spouse, children, or friends. Do something that is spontaneous—it will bring you pleasure.

POSITION 3: You expect someone not to fulfill a promise and you will be right. This is one of life's little problems that comes up regularly. Your husband promises to cut the grass but doesn't. Your son tells you that he will be home by midnight but isn't. Your co-worker promises to find the information but doesn't. We get angry and a bigger problem is created. As long as we can keep the matter in perspective, that it is a minor breach of promise, no real harm will be done.

POSITION 4: An obstacle with which you will have to fight. The problem or obstacle is slightly more serious than that indicated by the picture in position 3, but again nothing major. Obstacles in life are a challenge. When we overcome them, we get a powerful sense of achievement. Like the farmer, we don't have to kill the birds that invade our fields; we can learn to outwit them by using a scarecrow or noise. Likewise, look at the obstacle and think of creative ways to overcome it. That way you can save your energy for real problems.

13 BOY

PERIOD OF INFLUENCE: immediate to short

SYMBOL FOR: adventure

MEANING: ↓ 1. Travel in the near future.
 → 2. You will find yourself in pleasant company and
    will have a good time.
 ← 3. A new friendship is possible.
 ↑ 4. An unexpected meeting or a date.

GENERAL MEANING OF PICTURE: The boy signifies youth,
energy, adventure. Whether we are young or not, the picture refers to
our childish sense of adventure or playfulness. It is the time to behave
like a young boy; to trust new people and look for the adventure in
everyday things. We need to let go of our adult roles at times and seek
the simple pleasures that we used to enjoy as youths.

POSITION 1: Travel is possible in the near future. This is a very
good time to take a trip to anywhere you desire. Even if you have not
planned on taking a trip at this time, but something unexpected
happens and you have the opportunity to go, then do so, as a good
time is indicated. This does not have to be an expensive trip; rather, it
can be one of discovery, of seeing new places and situations from a
different perspective than we normally would. It can be a camping
trip to Hawaii, a walking trip to Katmandu, a stay at a pension in
Rome, or snorkeling in the Great Barrier Reef. A soccer exchange to
another city with your children may be a lesser adventure, but a
memorable one nevertheless. Wherever you go, you will go with the
sense of adventure that a boy has on discovering something new.

60

POSITION 2: You will find yourself in pleasant company and will have a good time. This can be an unexpected gathering of people or something already planned. You will feel like a schoolkid, free of cares and worries. You can relax and enjoy yourself, as everyone feels the same way and there will be no repercussions the next day. The picture may refer to your immediate state—that is, if you are doing the reading with a group of friends. Usually the picture stimulates conversation and everyone has a good time.

POSITION 3: A new friendship is possible. This is important as many of us do not make new friends easily after a certain age. When this picture shows up, take a good look around you to see who this new friend could be. It could be an acquaintance, a neighbor, someone completely new, or an old friend from the past who enters the scene again. Be yourself, so that when you come in contact with the new friend, you have the basis for a strong friendship.

The new friend could also be someone younger than you. It is important to keep communications open to people younger and older than you. Having friends of various ages gives you different perspectives on life and keeps you from boredom. Also, as you age, friends begin to disappear, so it is a good idea to make new ones. Recent research is showing that people who have sound relationships with friends and family live longer and more happily.

POSITION 4: An unexpected meeting or a date. This could simply be running into an old friend, co-worker, neighbor, or an old flame. However, the picture can also mean that someone will call you unexpectedly for a date. In either case you will have an enjoyable time. The picture could also refer to running into someone who has inflicted pain or hurt you in some way in the past. However, when they see you, you will be at your best, surprising them. You will get a childish sense of pleasure at having conquered your fears and hurts and being able to see the other person objectively.

14 FOX

PERIOD OF INFLUENCE: short

SYMBOL FOR: deceit

MEANING: ↓ 1. You are being cunningly deceived.
→ 2. A falsity will be revealed.
← 3. It isn't wise to trust a new friendship.
↑ 4. Be careful not to feel unwarranted trust toward some people.

GENERAL MEANING OF PICTURE: The fox is an animal that we associate with cunning and deceit. The fox doesn't come out during the day to catch its prey, but sneaks around at night, when everyone is asleep, to do its work. Basically, the fox does not do any more damage than other carnivores, but it gets its reputation by the means it uses. The fox in Aesop's fable "The Fox and the Crow" uses flattery to make the crow drop its cheese. These are the people who will use any method available, fair or not, to reach their goal. Thus the picture warns you of people who are like the fox, sly and crafty. They are not necessarily out to hurt you; rather, they are after their own self-preservation. You can't avoid such individuals, but can learn to outwit them and minimize the damage they cause.

POSITION 1: You are being cunningly deceived. This could refer to your spouse cheating on you, your child using drugs and hiding it from you, your fellow employee taking credit for what you did, or your being taken in by a business transaction that is dishonest. In all cases the other person is doing it intentionally, knowing that he or she is not being honest with you. The person might not intend to hurt you but simply be caught up in the situation and take the easiest way out. For example, a husband cheating on his wife is so caught up in the excitement of the moment that he has little time to consider his actions. When this picture comes up, pay particular attention to those around you, to see who is deceiving you and why. Sometimes it isn't easy to discover who is deceiving you, as that person is working in a sly manner. Even if you don't discover the deceit, be circumspect in all your actions, as you know there is someone you should not trust.

POSITION 2: A falsity will be disclosed. This could be something that you have lied or made a mistake about, or something that someone else has lied or made a mistake about. The Russians say: Lies have short legs. In other words, lies can't go far; they are soon discovered. If it is you who has made the mistake or lied, then admit your mistake openly and take the consequences. You will suffer less in the long run if you admit to your mistakes. If the mistake or lie has been made by someone else, then accept it graciously and work together to straighten it out. Don't gloat over other people's mistakes, as you never know when you might be in the same situation.

POSITION 3: Don't be too trustful with a new friendship. The BOY picture tells you of a new friendship. If that picture appears, then you can trust the new friend with any information you wish to share. However, if the FOX picture comes up in this position, then be careful with the new friend. The new friend may be someone who has joined your social circle, your work place, or your recreational activity. It is someone you will most likely be seeing on a regular basis; so you will have to be on guard. Don't share any private ideas, opinions, or actions with this person. Be especially careful when drinking, as your tongue can become loose and you may divulge more than you intended. The new friend may be a nice person, someone you really like, but you must be aware that this person's first concern is his or her own welfare. He or she might use in a detrimental way any information obtained from you.

POSITION 4: Don't be too trustful with some people around you. This broadens the circle of people from that referred to by the picture in the previous position. The picture could be warning you against someone in your family or your work place, among your business acquaintances, or even in your neighborhood. It is not so much danger that you have to be aware of, as it is deceit. You will have to look at other pictures in the reading to see what kind of loss you may suffer—emotional, monetary, or business. As mentioned previously for this picture, when you get it, be very careful of information that you divulge.

The picture also can refer to information that you divulge to your boss or government officials. You should not lie, but you don't have to divulge more than is necessary. Remember that it is the job of officials to catch people on technicalities, so don't place unwarranted trust in everyone at this time.

If you are starting a business, you should be particularly careful in what you are doing, as there are hidden dangers.

15 BEAR

PERIOD OF INFLUENCE: middle

SYMBOL FOR: work, effort, with good results

MEANING: ↓ 1. With caution, happiness will not elude you.
        → 2. Your efforts will bear fruit.
        ← 3. You will get what you desire, although not in the immediate future.
        ↑ 4. Don't have faith in every piece of advice.

GENERAL MEANING OF PICTURE: The bear is our inborn brute strength and resilience. At a certain time in human evolution, the bear was worshiped, perhaps for its tremendous strength. However, a bear does not depend only on its strength to kill for food, but can also consume berries, catch fish, and even find ingenious ways of obtaining honey. Having filled itself, a bear can hibernate during cold, lean times. The early cave men and women had to lead lives similar to that of the bear. It is understandable that they would worship the survival instincts of the bear. The picture tells us to be like the bear, to trust and follow our natural instincts for survival, which include knowing when and where to seek sustenance and when to lie low.

POSITION 1: With caution, happiness will not elude you. What you want is out there and can be obtained by you. It will bring you happiness as well, but you must be careful. Don't rush in, as cautioned by the old proverb "Fools rush in where angels fear to tread." Be like the bear: look the situation over, check for any traps, and only then go for the desired objective. The picture usually deals with aspects relating to your basic survival, which would include such things as your job, business, or any projects that will in the long run make your life more comfortable.

POSITION 2: Your efforts will bear fruit. Again, like the bear, you must work and exert effort in obtaining what you desire. A bear cannot afford to stay put and expect to survive. It must go looking for food. In the same way, you must seek your fortune and exert extra effort. We laugh at the image of a bear, out on a limb, its face covered with bees, yet its paw reaching for the beehive that contains the nectar of the gods, honey. The bear knows that the reward is worth the effort. So it is for you: if you want something, you can· get it, but it does require extra effort on your part. The reward is that you will get what you are working toward.

The reward for your efforts might not appear immediately. For example, raising children is an effort that goes on for a long time. Parenting is also made difficult by all the pressures that are put on children by advertising, television, and peers. How can you serve them hot oatmeal for breakfast when every other child in the world is eating Sugar Loops or some other latest concoction? The picture advises you to follow your instincts regardless of the objections of the little ones. The reward will be that your children will grow up to be healthy, well-adjusted individuals.

POSITION 3: You will get what you desire, but not in the immediate future. The picture tells you to be patient. Although you want to do something, the time isn't right for it at present. Don't get discouraged and abandon the project; realize that perhaps you need further experience or information before your project can be the success that it is meant to be. This picture appeared for me many times during the writing of this book. I was impatient to finish the project, yet every time I was stopped, I gained further understanding of how the cards work. Had the first effort been published, it would have contained inadequate information. So bide your time, knowing that each positive or negative experience is a learning process that will make your ultimate objective more worthwhile.

POSITION 4: Don't trust every piece of advice—including the advice of the cards. What this means is that there are many worthwhile paths in life to follow, but not every one is meant for us. The picture tells you to trust your own gut reaction regarding what is right and what is not for you. A friend was told that he had cancer. Rather than follow the conventional methods of surgery and radiation only, he investigated and found that there were many holistic approaches to curing cancer. He vigorously pursued every piece of advice that came his way, with the result that he lost a great deal of weight and in fact was under more stress. The picture came up for him in this position, warning him that all advice was not necessarily good for him. We have to rely on our own instincts and act on them rather than following the advice of everyone else. The friend chose those treatments that he liked the best and eliminated the rest. The result was that he eliminated unnecessary stress and two years later was cancer-free.

16 STARS

PERIOD OF INFLUENCE: short to life

SYMBOL FOR: destiny influencing your life

MEANING: ↓ 1. Your guiding star will bring you to your goal.
→ 2. Success in dealings.
← 3. Temporary blindness will force you to make a series of mistakes.
↑ 4. A series of unpleasant occurrences.

GENERAL MEANING OF PICTURE: This picture is for dreamers, for people who feel they have to accomplish something in life. They can be artists, sculptors, architects, writers, politicians, or anyone who has a dream or ambitions. Not only their own efforts but also the influence of heavenly bodies will make their dreams come true.

POSITION 1: Your guiding star will bring you to your goal. Your ambitions will be realized. This does not mean right away or without effort on your part. The picture is always an inspiration, telling you not to give up on your dreams. Like the early navigators who used the stars to guide them to their destinations, so you should pursue your goals. If you do so, you will attain them in your lifetime.

POSITION 2: Success in dealings. The heavenly bodies are working for you, making your deals succeed. This refers to everyday matters in your life. Whatever you are pursuing will meet with success. It could be that your goals are becoming reality, or that you are fulfilling chapters in your life that ultimately will lead you to your goal.

POSITION 3: Temporary blindness will force you to make a series of mistakes. This is like the navigator who makes a wrong reading of the stars and then has to spend time getting back to the original course. This is not a bad picture, but it warns of unpleasantness usually due to your own errors. Temporary blindness can refer to states of anger, jealousy, fear, or anything that causes you to become self-absorbed and unaware of people and circumstances around you. The mistakes that result are not major ones, like those warned of by the MOUNTAIN or HEARSE pictures. You could lock your keys in the car, hand in the wrong assignment, go to the wrong address, or make some other mistake of this magnitude. The warning lasts for about a week or two and could already apply when you are doing the reading.

POSITION 4: A series of unpleasant occurrences. These again are not serious but nevertheless are unpleasant. This can refer to mistakes at work, unpleasant remarks, missed schedules or appointments, running out of supplies. It usually refers to occurrences that are out of your control. You should be aware that life is not smooth right now. Brace yourself for small annoying problems. Being aware that problems are likely makes you better prepared to face and solve them. This is not a time to get upset over minor difficulties. The early sea captains had to face unfriendly natives, rats, and scurvy, yet they were still able to reach their destinations.

17 HERON

PERIOD OF INFLUENCE: middle

SYMBOL FOR: new beginnings, change

MEANING: ↓ 1. A change in place of residence.
           → 2. Circumstances will force you to enter an undesirable path.
           ← 3. A change in relations with friends.
           ↑ 4. An addition to the family.

GENERAL MEANING OF PICTURE: The stork, a relative of the heron, is traditionally associated with the arrival of newborn babies. The HERON has this meaning in position 4. Both the heron and the stork also symbolize unexpected occurrences in and around our homes. The heron is a long-legged bird that lives in marshes and along river banks. It catches fish and even can be used by humans to do the same. To have herons near your house was once considered lucky as it indicated there were fish, a source of food, close by. Herons have been known to build their nests on chimney tops during the summer months. In the fall, when the fireplace is lit, the smoke cannot escape due to the nest. The house fills up with smoke and soot. Thus unexpected turmoil, havoc, and confusion result. Upon the arrival of a newborn baby, there is also confusion and disarray as we try to adjust to a new situation. The HERON is not a negative picture, but one that warns you of unexpected changes occurring around your home.

POSITION 1: A change of residence is probable at this time. It does not mean that you have to move, only that the circumstances are

70

good for a change of residence at this time. If you are thinking of buying a house, then the deal you are making is good, and you should go ahead with it. The same would apply to any other type of residence. There are times in your life when you consider moving into a larger house or buying one for investment purposes. However, you hesitate and don't go through with it. Later you look back and regret not having purchased the property. Everything has appreciated and you would have done very well financially. Hindsight is great, but unless you do something at the appropriate time you will have regrets. When the picture appears in this position, you shouldn't hesitate. Problems will work out and the move will be a successful one. Remember herons have to move to where the fish are.

POSITION 2: Circumstances will force you to enter an undesirable path. Like the heron that builds a nest on your chimney and forces you to clean your house of smoke and soot, so circumstances will force you to do something you don't like. It could relate to staying in a relationship you are unhappy in because you have no financial means of escaping at this time. Or it could mean being forced to leave a secure environment despite your wishes. The actions of other people may also force you on a new path. Children leave home or marry, creating an "empty nest." You are powerless to change the circumstances. Go along with what is demanded of you at this time. This picture influences your life for only one to a few months, so you know there will be an end to your frustrations. A Russian proverb applies here: "I might as well enjoy the ride," said the parrot as it was being dragged by the cat.

POSITION 3: A change in relations with friends. This can either mean that you will renew your friendship or that you will drift apart. In either case it is usually due to external circumstances over which you have no control. Friends may move away, break up, or have new happenings in their lives that will affect your relationship with them. When this happens, the thing to remember is not to feel betrayed or abandoned but to accept it as part of our modern lifestyle. Perhaps in the future, circumstances will change and the friendship will be reestablished.

POSITION 4: An addition to the family. If a young couple gets this picture, then it signifies a pregnancy or arrival of a newborn baby.

However, the picture also comes up for people who are past child-bearing years or those not interested in having children. For those people, the picture indicates that someone will be joining their household. This could be a child coming back, a relative, or even a friend. It does not mean that this person will be staying with you forever, only that he or she will stay with you until your or the person's needs are fulfilled. For example, a child is coming home for the summer holidays, or you will rent out your spare bedroom. In either case, your family will expand, and this expansion will bring with it all the joy, turmoil, and confusion that a newborn baby brings to a household.

18 DOG

PERIOD OF INFLUENCE: middle to life

SYMBOL FOR: relationships with friends

MEANING: ↓ 1. You have a faithful and constant friend.
          → 2. The help of friends will support you.
          ← 3. A person you consider a friend is untrue to you.
          ↑ 4. A change of friends.

GENERAL MEANING OF PICTURE: The dog is humankind's best friend. Thus the DOG picture symbolizes our best friend. The friend can be a family member, a spouse, or any other friend we have.

POSITION 1: You have a faithful and constant friend. The value of this picture is not so much to tell you that which you already know, but to remind you that you have friends you can rely on for help. Your friends are faithful to you. For example, you had planned to do some traveling with a friend but the plans fell through, and you are inclined to put the blame on your friend. Then this picture comes up in position 1. This is a gentle reminder that your friend was not at fault. On further consideration, you will realize that you were partially to blame for the plans' not going through. In fact, your friend was a better friend to you than you were to him or her.

POSITION 2: You have friends whom you can rely on. When going through life's difficult moments we have friends who are willing to help us, and we should allow them to do so. Not all people are good, but when you get this picture, you know the people around you can be depended upon and trusted. Other pictures such as the FOREST in positions 3 and 4, the CAT, FOX, and HORSE will warn you of danger from friends. The word *friend* is interesting. Sometimes we get the greatest support from people whom we don't even consider as close friends. For example, during a difficult time in your life, a friend of your spouse's may somehow sense your trouble and by inviting you out to social gatherings help you get through your immediate crisis. The death of someone in your family usually brings out unexpected support from friends. A friend may bring over a pie or some other food, knowing that cooking is not on your mind at the time, yet it is necessary to eat to maintain strength. You might even hear from friends that you haven't seen for a long time. The fact is that there are people out there who care for you. This picture is always welcome as it reminds you that you are not alone in this big world. The Russian proverb says: Better to have a hundred friends than a hundred rubles.

POSITION 3: In position 3, the picture is more negative. A person you consider a friend is untrue to you. This generally implies that you have put more into a friendship than the other person has. You might consider someone a friend, while he or she considers you one of many acquaintances. Your feelings are not considered at any great depth by this person. Also, friendships do undergo strains. Perhaps your friend has turned away from you over some real or imagined hurt. The important thing is to realize that you have a friend who is not as close to you as you wish, and that you should not be as trustful as you would normally be. The situation is out of your hands and there is nothing you can do about it, so just be wary of too much confidence. The HANDSHAKE is another picture that deals with friendship. If it comes up, it will tell you to put effort into keeping a friendship alive, while this picture just tells you what the situation is. Interestingly enough, when this picture comes up, the person whose cards are being read usually knows immediately who this untrue friend is.

POSITION 4: A change in friendship is occurring. It is sad to get this picture as it usually signals a change of friendship for the worse—that is, the parting of friends. However, it could also mean the intensification of a friendship. The change is due to uncontrollable events such as finishing school, or devoting more time to marriage, children, or work. It is sad when this happens, but in some cases it is a temporary situation and the intensity of the friendship might resume at some later date. The important thing is to remember what you got from the friendship. You may remember the close bond, the sharing of ideals and future plans, that you established with someone at school. Now you have finished and have gone your separate ways. It is sad that this friendship has ended, yet on looking back, you can see how much your life was enriched by it.

19 CASTLE

PERIOD OF INFLUENCE: life

SYMBOL FOR: security

MEANING: ↓ 1. Fulfillment of hopes, although at the end of your life.
→ 2. A refuge in old age.
← 3. A long life.
↑ 4. A chronic illness.

GENERAL MEANING OF PICTURE: The castle is material security. A castle has always meant safety and protection from one's enemies. Traditionally it referred to a heavily walled building, fortified to protect the inhabitants from enemy attack. As civilization progressed, people no longer needed the strong fortification, but the idea of safety and refuge has remained. The saying "A home is a person's castle" still has meaning today. A castle had to be built using sound methods in order to be a place of safety. Likewise, a home can be a refuge only if one puts in enough time and effort to make it a comfortable place. Thus the meaning of this picture is that one will get one's just rewards, but it is due to one's earnest efforts in life and not to chance. In the past, a strong castle provided security and the opportunity to live one's natural life to the end. The picture is a life picture—that is, its prediction spans your life. It represents those aspects of your life that will provide an optimum environment for you to live in.

POSITION 1: Whatever your hopes in life are, they will be fulfilled, even if at the end of your life. If you are seeking a happy relationship, a home, a publisher for your book, travel to an exotic place, or the like, your hopes will be realized, although perhaps not as soon as you would wish. The problem is that many of us want it sooner than is ordained. We don't want to wait a lifetime; after all, this is the age of instant gratification. The picture tells you to relax, stop trying so hard, keep on working toward your goal, don't rush it. You will get what you want, but later. The irony is that if you get it too soon, it might be the end of your life as well.

A castle does not only mean security. A castle is a safe refuge, yet if we confine ourselves to it, the results might not be to our benefit in the long run. The Tower of London is an example of a refuge turned to a prison. During the Middle Ages, a moat was built around the tower for further protection. The moat was connected to the Thames River for drainage. However, the drainage didn't work well and for more than four hundred years, the moat was a cesspool. The inhabitants of the tower were exposed to all kinds of diseases. It was Queen Victoria who finally had the moat filled in and restored health to the inhabitants of the tower. The moral of the story is that what we think we want might not be good for us in the long run. The picture tells you, you will get your wish but don't rush it. Smell the roses along the way. You might have a fuller life than you expected. The Russians say: The quieter you travel, the farther you'll get. Those who are always in a hurry not only miss many details and have to redo them later, but also increase their chance of dying young from high blood pressure. Therefore, strive for your goals, but be patient; you will get as far as you want to go.

POSITION 2: You will have a secure place in old age. This should be a comfort to those who are going through rough times at present, to know that their problems will get resolved and they won't be destitute in old age. A friend who had recently gone through her second divorce and lost her third house got this picture. It was comforting for her to know that life would straighten itself out and she would have a secure place in old age. Knowing this, she could take more chances rather than being paralyzed with fear of the future.

If you are only in your twenties or thirties and you have already created a refuge for yourself, maybe you should take some chances now; otherwise, your refuge can lead to boredom if you attain it at too early an age.

POSITION 3: A long life. This does not mean that you can take foolish chances or not take care of yourself. A castle can deteriorate or be captured by the enemy if one is not careful. In the same way, you have to be protective of your health and environment to ensure that you will live out your years. A healthy lifestyle with work, relaxation, and enjoyment of family and friends leads to longevity. The picture is reassuring in that it implies that what you are doing for your health and welfare is positive and will lead you to a long life.

POSITION 4: Something in your life is wrong, with the result that you have a chronic illness. Castles were often cold and drafty places; although they protected the people, they could make them ill as well. People had to wear extra clothes and cover the walls and windows with tapestries for protection from the cold. In the same way, you might have an ailment that will stay with you for your lifetime. You have to find means to deal with it—perhaps not cure it, but keep it at bay so that you can still lead a productive life. Sometimes by taking care of ourselves because we have a chronic illness, we can lead longer and better lives. As an example, a friend has had gallstones for over twenty years and has had to watch her diet all the time, avoiding fatty foods. Recent medical findings say that fatty foods are the leading cause of heart attacks and cancer. So by taking care of one ailment, perhaps my friend has avoided more dangerous illnesses. The picture warns you that whatever precautions you are taking will have to be strictly followed at this time of your life.

It is also a good idea to examine your lifestyle and see if some of your habits are contributing to the chronic illness. Are you smoking or drinking too much, not exercising enough, working too hard, isolating yourself? Perhaps this is a good time to shore up your castle walls by undertaking some long-range changes.

20 FOREST

PERIOD OF INFLUENCE: middle

SYMBOL FOR: people around you

MEANING: ↓ 1. Continuous friendship with many worthwhile people.
→ 2. Mixing with a purpose in numerous and agreeable society.
← 3. Contact with suspicious people.
↑ 4. Beware of the nets that are thrown your way.

GENERAL MEANING OF PICTURE: A forest is made up of many trees. It has weathered storms, fires, animals, parasites, and anything else that nature has thrust upon it. Yet the trees stand, giving protection to their neighbors, and in turn being protected by them. In the same way, we do not stand alone. We are surrounded by people. The picture refers to people who have grown up with you or who have shared experiences of a growing nature. For the most part, these people are helping you, as indicated by the picture in the first two positions. However, there are times when you have to beware of the people around you, which the picture indicates in the last two positions.

POSITION 1: Continuous friendship with many worthwhile people. The card tells you that you have made friends with people who are of good character. They are a good influence in your life. Your shared interests will be a support and an inspiration to you. The people can include those you work with, live with, or have as friends.

The picture quite often appears when you are in transition—that is, changing from one stage in your life to another. This could be a change of residence, careers, jobs, becoming single again, or the like. The picture is a reminder that you have established strong bonds that will remain in spite of the changes that are going on in your life. The picture further tells you that your friends will be there should you need them. These are not frivolous friends who disappear when the goodies are gone. Rather, they are friends who nurture you, as you nurture them back also.

POSITION 2: Mixing with a purpose in numerous and agreeable society. This is a good picture for socially mobile people. If you want to get ahead in your job, then you are in the right company or society to help you advance. If you are single, then you are in the right gathering to meet a prospective partner. The picture tells you that whatever activities you are doing are good for you. At the same time, you are having a good time.

If you are not doing much socializing, then the picture urges you to get out and do something. Volunteer for the Red Cross, join a political group, enroll in an aerobics class, or get involved in any activity that interests you. There are times in life when you benefit by being part of a social group rather then being alone.

The picture may refer to the people you are doing the reading with. Their contributions to the discussion are valuable and worth noting.

POSITION 3: Contact with suspicious people. When this picture appears, beware of people around you. They may want something that you have. In the forest, when a new tree begins to grow, it is in competition with its neighbors for light, water, and soil. Be aware of your rights and don't be too trusting at this time.

The picture also may be warning you of dangerous people around you. Your instincts will tell you who to beware of. The suspicious people are doing something illegal or dishonest, either consciously or unconsciously. Here we have to include people whose personalities change radically when using drugs or alcohol.

The picture began appearing for me several years ago when I was teaching a particular group. A series of unpleasant incidents happened. These were not the pranks of ordinary students but malicious acts. Since that time, one of those students has been arrested, while another has been put into a mental institution. The picture was a warning to me to be careful with the people around me. I always followed the advice, did not do anything to aggravate the situation, and came out intact. Should the picture appear again, I will know to be careful.

If you are in a new situation such as a job or sharing accommodations with new people, then be particularly careful. The new people may not be honest.

POSITION 4: Beware of the nets that are thrown your way. People want you to do something that is for their benefit but not yours. It could be as serious as getting you involved with breaking the law, for which you will get caught. Or it could be getting you involved in some project from which you will not benefit but which will demand a lot of your time and effort.

Be particularly careful about signing any documents at this time. They will be worded in such a way as to benefit the other party and not you. Once you have signed, you will find it hard to make changes in the future.

Also be particularly careful in family relationships. Your partner may be trying to trap you, to make you take the blame for something that he or she is responsible for.

At work, do your job well. Don't give others a chance to sabotage or criticize your work by leaving anything undone or unfinished. Protect your home base.

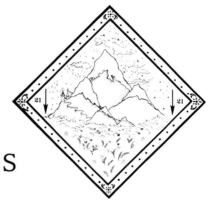

21 MOUNTAINS

PERIOD OF INFLUENCE: immediate

SYMBOL FOR: danger

MEANING: ↓ 1. A treacherous enemy is trying to catch you, be on guard.
→ 2. Nearness to a great unpleasantness that can be avoided.
← 3. After deliberation you will make the right decision.
↑ 4. You will receive help from strong people during a difficult moment.

GENERAL MEANING OF PICTURE: This is one of the stronger pictures and should be paid attention to. It warns of danger that comes from the outside, not something that we have created ourselves. The mountains are nature's largest creations. They can be both a restriction and a protection to humankind. Scaling mountains has always involved danger, yet humans continue to strive to conquer the natural forces. In the first two positions, the picture warns of danger, while in the last two positions it tells you that natural forces will come to your aid.

POSITION 1: A treacherous enemy is trying to catch you; be on guard. Beware of people around you. A co-worker could be after your job, or your boss could be looking for an excuse to fire you. A burglar is casing your home, looking for an opportune time to break in. A spouse is looking for an excuse to leave you. The picture is not meant to make you paranoid, but it does warn of a danger at this particular time. This is not the time to relax or be slothful. It is a time to do your best at work and at home, so that no one can catch you unawares.

Sometimes we are not aware of people who mean to do us harm. When the picture comes up, take a closer look at the people around you to see who the enemy might be. You don't have to do anything, just be careful around that person.

POSITION 2: Nearness to a great unpleasantness that can be avoided. Generally, the picture warns you of physical danger. The picture came up for me once; shortly after, while driving on a freeway, my brakes failed. I was lucky that I was on a flat stretch of road and was able to stop without causing an accident. When this picture comes up, fix all your broken appliances, have your car looked over, and fix anything that could cause an accident. Also be careful about climbing ladders or roofs, lighting barbecues, starting boats, going near mean dogs, and so forth. This is not a time to be negligent. By being careful, you can avoid danger.

POSITION 3: After deliberation you will make the right decision. The picture is very encouraging in this position. It is telling you to evaluate your situation; test the negative aspects against the positive ones and decide which ones are more important to you. You can write out the pros and cons of a situation. By seeing the information on the paper, you can make a better choice. Sometimes even though the negative points are much more numerous than the positive ones, you may decide that the few positive points outweigh all the negative ones. This system can be used for personal problems, or financial and business matters.

The point of the picture is to take time in making decisions. Like the mountains, the decisions are important, and they should be given due consideration. In the process you will find out your real values.

POSITION 4: You will receive help from strong people during a difficult moment. Some influential or strong persons are willing to help you. The help may be in the form of personal contact or behind the scenes. This is the opposite of the meaning when the picture is in position 1, warning you to beware of people. In position 4, the picture means that if you have problems at work, it is a good time to seek the advice of your superiors. If you have personal problems and can't solve them, then it might be a good time to talk to a psychiatrist, doctor, minister, counselor, or someone who can put your problems in a proper perspective. Sometimes the help may come from people whom you least expect to be strong or supportive. The Russians have a lovely proverb: Friends in need get to know each other.

You may not even be aware of the help you are receiving. People that have power such as lawyers, agents, supervisors and such are promoting you and your work, working to get you the best deal that is possible. The picture in this position tells you to trust your business associates and managers.

22 ROAD

PERIOD OF INFLUENCE: middle to life

SYMBOL FOR: path in life

MEANING: ↓ 1. Happy path or road.
         → 2. A joyful journey.
         ← 3. A lonely and boring road or work.
         ↑ 4. Difficulties on the road.

GENERAL MEANING OF PICTURE: The road symbolizes your path in life. The road ahead may be smooth, indicating that there are no major problems in your life at this time, or with the picture in the last two positions, the road may be less smooth. For those wishing to travel, this is one of the best pictures. In second position it not only indicates travel, but shows as well that it is going to be a joyful journey.

POSITION 1: Happy road. Your life is going great right now. Your work, home, recreation, and spiritual life are all on the right path.

If you are asking the cards whether you should travel at this time or not, then the picture tells you that this is definitely a good time to plan a trip. If you are doing a reading in January for the whole year, the picture tells you that a trip is in store for you during the year. One year three of us desperately wanted to go to Europe for the summer. The picture showed up for only one of us. One of the friends, who doesn't really believe in fortune telling, went ahead and planned her trip regardless of the fact that this picture didn't show up for her. A month before she was supposed to leave, her friends in England informed her that they were being moved back to Canada. Her trip had to be canceled. I also wanted to go, regardless of the cards, but found that unexpected obstacles—dental work—kept me from leaving. The one friend who had the picture show up had an unexpected death in the family and didn't know if she should go or not. Finally she decided to go. It was a fantastic holiday for her, and the situation at home worked out well in spite of her absence.

POSITION 2: An enjoyable journey; happy travels. The picture tells you that any travel plans you have will turn out well. Everything will go favorably and you will have a fantastic time. The trip could be a major one, such as going to Europe, Asia, or Africa; or it could be a short trip to the cottage, a fishing trip, or a shopping expedition to the nearest big center.

If you are not traveling, the picture indicates that everything in your life is going smoothly and flowing the way it should. In fact, life seems like a party right now. Everything you are doing is enjoyable, bringing joy and happiness.

POSITION 3: A lonely and boring road or work. Your life is placid at this time. This is like the months of January and February; after the holidays and before spring. You are doing your chores or work but getting bored with it. This is not a bad picture to get, it just indicates dissatisfaction with your lot at this time. However, you should realize that quiet times are restful to the soul and body. We need them just as much as we need fun and excitement.

If you are working on a long-term objective when the picture comes up, then think of creative ways to animate your work. Just remember that Rome wasn't built in a day. Any great accomplishment takes many, many hours of effort.

However, if the picture refers to your life in general, if everything is boring to you, then you should evaluate your life at this time. Perhaps you have forgotten your dreams or goals in the mundane tasks of your everyday life. If you are a homemaker, than maybe you should think of going back to school or work. If you are bored with your job, then perhaps you should look for a new job or even think of switching careers. You are given one shot at life, so don't waste it being bored.

POSITION 4: Difficulties on the road. If the picture refers to your everyday life, then you will have obstacles to contend with. This could be problems at work or at home that you have to overcome. This is not a bad picture, it just means that life sometimes challenges us and we have to face it. Overcoming problems adds to our self-esteem and self-respect. Therefore, we should not fear them but should feel challenged to do our best.

If the picture refers to travel, then you will have difficulties on the trip. These are not major problems, but minor annoyances. Your baggage may be lost, a mix-up with hotels may happen, delays may occur, and so forth. Having been forewarned of problems, you will be better prepared to face them. The main part of the trip need not be spoiled.

23 MICE

PERIOD OF INFLUENCE: immediate

SYMBOL FOR: loss or finding of material article

MEANING: ↓ 1. You will find what you have lost.
　　　　　→ 2. An unexpected discovery.
　　　　　← 3. A theft.
　　　　　↑ 4. The stolen goods have disappeared forever.

GENERAL MEANING OF PICTURE: Mice are industrious little animals that exist on what they can forage or steal around the house. Thus the MICE picture symbolizes the loss or finding of material goods. It is a relatively minor picture, unless what you have lost is of value to you. The picture is helpful in that it tells you whether to exert energy searching for the object or not.

POSITION 1: You will find what you have lost. This is a reassuring picture. Quite often when we lose something, we get in a frenzy searching for it and ruin our chance of finding the article. The picture tells you that you will find it. Take it easy. Think methodically where it could be or where it could have fallen to. If you have lost something in a public place, then advertise the loss or report it to an authority who can help you find it. If you are patient, the chances are good that you will retrieve the lost article.

A friend of mine had lost her gold charm bracelet. She had looked everywhere and was convinced that it had been either stolen or lost forever. However, the MICE picture kept coming up for her. Finally, after more than a year, she found the bracelet in some old clothing she was ready to give to charity.

POSITION 2: An unexpected discovery. This may refer to finding something of value that you had completely forgotten you had. It could be a piece of jewelry, money, uncashed bonds, or anything that pleases you.

The picture may also refer to finding something of value that is not yours. Make an effort to return it. You will be rewarded either immediately or in life generally. A funny incident happened in our family to illustrate this point. One day a cat walked into our house and made himself at home. My son wanted to keep him as a partner to our own cat. However, I told him to check the lost-and-found section of the paper as the owner might be looking for his pet. Sure enough, there was an ad. The owner rushed over. He was so happy that he gave my son a fifty-dollar reward. What an easy lesson this was for my son to learn! He saw that by returning what he had found, he made the other person extremely happy as well as pocketing the reward himself.

POSITION 3: A theft. Don't leave valuable goods lying around as they may be taken in the same way that mice eat food that is left out. Make sure your doors are locked and the locks work properly. This is not a time to be careless with your possessions. Jewelry, cameras, bikes, and all such objects should be safely put away so that they are not a temptation to anyone. Be careful of the people around you and don't venture into unknown territory. Theft or robbery is possible. Remember, thieves don't like to be caught. Therefore, by taking preventive measures, you may avoid the theft.

POSITION 4: The stolen goods have disappeared forever. Whatever has been stolen or lost is gone forever. If the article has personal value to you, you have to let go of wishing for it, as it is gone forever. Your mother's ring may have been stolen, but your memories of your mother will stay with you forever.

You may or may not get compensated by your insurance company for your loss. Many years ago while we were camping in Hawaii, our car with all its contents was stolen. Due to a technicality, the insurance company did not reimburse us. We tried various means of getting the insurance, but nothing worked. When the picture began coming up in this position, I knew it was time to give up. I was wasting my energy, as the insurance company would not budge. Even though to this day I believe the company was wrong, it was easier to absorb the loss than to continue to fight a losing battle.

24 HEART

PERIOD OF INFLUENCE: middle

SYMBOL FOR: love

MEANING: ↓ 1. Your happiness is in the answer of the person you love.
→ 2. Love will ignite your heart.
← 3. Merriment, gaiety, will never leave you.
↑ 4. You are in agreement with close people.

GENERAL MEANING OF PICTURE: The heart has been a symbol of love for thousands of years. In recent times, with all the publicity that heart transplants have received, we know that the heart is life itself. A wonderful blending of these meanings is to say that by loving, we give life to our lives. But love is more than that of a man and a woman. It can also be the love for our parents, children, country, work, or anything that deeply touches our feelings, which we call the heart. It is always sad to see people searching for love, the romantic kind, and at the same time ignoring the love extended to them by their children, family, or friends. The HEART picture gives guidance to the emotions that we say come from the heart.

POSITION 1: Your happiness is in the answer of the person you love. In this position, the picture is somewhat negative, in that it tells you that a love relationship depends not only on your being in love, but also on the other person's reciprocating. It usually implies that the other person is not aware of your feelings or does not feel as passionate about the relationship as you do at this time. This is the time to redouble your efforts to be attractive, loving, and giving in order to ignite the passion in your partner. Demanding love will not work, but gentle, subtle means will help. This is the time for cozy romantic dinners, perfume, music, flowers, and lots of time and attention for each other. If you want to be treated lovingly, then model the behavior for your partner.

If this is your first love and the other person doesn't even know you exist, don't despair. Double your efforts to be noticed, as the picture does indicate that love is a possibility. However, if none of your efforts succeed, then take solace in the Russian proverb: First love is like first teeth, it comes with pain.

POSITION 2: Love will ignite your heart. This generally means the passionate type of love. It can mean that the man or woman of your dreams will appear and sweep you off your feet. Or it can also mean that your love for someone you already know can be rekindled to passionate intensity. Success or good times often stir our emotions, with the result that we experience strong surges of love. These feelings are natural and we should enjoy them, whether they are toward those around us or someone new. The picture tells you that love will ignite your heart, and that is all. The feeling of love is what is important, not what you might do physically. The picture doesn't give you license to go and have sexual intercourse with anyone you might have strong loving emotions toward. That is another matter that you have to decide on. However, the picture does tell you to enjoy the emotional aspect of loving someone.

POSITION 3: No matter what problems you will encounter in life, joy and merriment will never leave you. This picture often appears when a person is having problems and everything looks bleak. The picture is a gentle reminder that the problems will pass or that they aren't as serious as we think they are. The picture should make you smile and lift up your spirits, with the result that you will have extra vigor and energy to face the world. It reminds you to look at your whole life, to look at the joys that you do have, rather than to get depressed over one problem. Love and merriment are all around us, we only have to open our eyes and hearts to see it.

If you are having problems in your love life, the following Russian proverb will make you laugh: Love isn't a potato; you can't throw it out the window. When you love someone, you are vulnerable to pain whether it is inflicted intentionally or not. Only in fairy tales do people live happily forever after. As an adult you have to deal with pain; you can't simply throw it away as you would a spoiled potato. If you look at the comical side, your problems won't seem as big.

POSITION 4: You are in agreement with close people. This means that the love you have for your family, close friends, and humankind is mutual. It is a reassurance that the love you are feeling is good in the universal sense. The old Russian proverb says: Love toward people is the best richness. Not only do you gain, but so do others.

25 RING

PERIOD OF INFLUENCE: middle

SYMBOL FOR: relationship between two people

MEANING: ↓ 1. A wedding or agreement.
→ 2. Engagement to a rich person.
← 3. An interruption of relations between lovers or friends.
↑ 4. A complete breakup between people in love.

GENERAL MEANING OF PICTURE: The ring is a symbol of the commitment of two people to a lasting relationship. It can be a traditional marriage or one of many new forms of relationship that are occurring today. In any case, it symbolizes the union of two people in one entity. This does not mean that each person loses his or her own personality or identity. Instead, by each retaining their own selves, they form a new union that is stronger than that of the two separate beings. In the cards, the ring usually refers to a relationship between a man and a woman who are in love. However, it can also refer to other strong relationships that a person has.

POSITION 1: The ring symbolizes the union of two people in a marriage or agreement. If the person whose cards are being read is single, then this picture says that this is a good time for marriage. If the person isn't involved in a relationship already, then it means that this is a good time to carefully look around you, because the possibility of meeting someone that you can fall in love with and marry are good. For those who are married, this picture means that this is a good period in your marriage, a time when you are truly one with your partner. Sometimes this picture appears to people who are in the

94

middle of serious marital problems. The picture tells you that what you are arguing about is worthwhile and that the resolution will lead to an even stronger marriage bond. It will move you to a new plateau in your relationship, past the seven-year itch, to a mutual understanding and appreciation of your union. For other strong relationships, it means that you are in agreement with the other person on important matters.

POSITION 2: Engagement to a rich person. This is good news to most people. It means that the person you are involved with is having a prosperous time and you will most likely benefit or be affected favorably. If you are single, then the person you will marry will be rich. If you are already married, your spouse will prosper. However, this picture does not mean that the person will always be rich and that all your material worries will be taken care of for the rest of your life. The future is changeable. The Russians say: Never disavow jail or a beggar's purse. You may end up as a beggar or in jail sometime in your life, although you never thought it possible.

Also remember that there is more than one way of being rich. It can be having more than you need or wanting less than you have. When you get this picture, you know that this is a good time for you, so enjoy it with your partner.

POSITION 3: An interruption of relations between lovers or friends. There are problems in your relationship with perhaps a cessation of intimacy. It is up to you to examine your relationship if this picture comes up. Obviously there are problems that must be resolved if you want to regain the intimacy you once had. Rather than sleepwalking, you have to look at the actions of your partner and yourself to determine what is going wrong. Sometimes people get so dependent on the union of the two that they forget who they were before and stop doing the things that made them attractive to the other person in the first place. It is easy for women to get so absorbed in the roles of mother and housewife that they forget to also be the enticing being they were before the children came. In the same way, it is hard for women to reconcile the image of the knight in shining armor whom they married, with the couch potato who is watching the football game on TV. The picture doesn't tell you to abandon your present interests and concerns but reminds you not to forget those aspects of your lives that made you attractive to each other in the first place.

You cannot change the other person, but you can work on yourself, so that you can rekindle your relationship if it is a worthwhile one.

POSITION 4: A complete breakup between lovers. The things that led you into a union are finished and do not hold the magic they once did. A glance across the room no longer stirs up the loving feelings it once did. In fact, usually other feelings such as hate, loathing, scorn, and disgust are stirred up. This can be the reaction of either one or both partners. The picture signifies the end of a union that once existed.

The picture, however, does not necessarily mean the end of a marriage or relationship. It signifies that this is a natural break and if there is going to be a divorce or separation, then this would be a good time to leave. A natural cycle of attraction, love, union, dissipation, and ending has occurred. However, it does not follow that divorce is imminent. Many couples stay together even though the love that first brought them together is gone. Some stay together for monetary reasons, some for security, and others for reasons only known to themselves.

Just because the love that first brought you together is gone, does not mean that you can't build a new love that can be stronger and more satisfying than the first passion. For example, the picture may begin to appear in a relationship after ten years, indicating that this may be a good time to end the union as there seem to be insurmountable problems. However, a wise person once said, "Remember, if you don't resolve your problems now, you will face them again ten years down the road with someone new." By resolving your problems now you can continue your marriage on a higher plane. Even actions like infidelity can be forgiven and forgotten when partners truly communicate with each other. By carefully analyzing problems and attitudes, a couple can find solutions. On the other hand, some couples reach the magic wall, then break up rather than helping each other to scale it. These people may be on their second or third marriages.

This picture came up for a couple who shortly after separated. They were apart for about a year, but finally went back together. Each had felt that they had missed out on the sexual revolution of the seventies and eighties. They had married young, had two children, and led quite satisfying but ordinary lives. The romance and excitement were gone, so they were quite unhappy with their marriage.

After separating, each tried to enjoy the single life. It didn't turn out to be as exciting as each thought it would be. They both realized that what they had had together was much more satisfying. Today their marriage is different but much stronger.

When you get this picture, whether to finish the relationship at a natural breaking point or use it as a learning stepping-stone is your free choice. That is the wonder of the cards; they tell you the situation, but it is up to you to choose your path.

26 BOOK

PERIOD OF INFLUENCE: short

SYMBOL FOR: secret news

MEANING: ↓ 1. Communication of a secret.
  → 2. Something that is of importance to you is being hidden from you.
  ← 3. A secret entrusted to you will be disclosed.
  ↑ 4. Your talkativeness will bring you harm.

GENERAL MEANING OF PICTURE: The book has always been associated with knowledge. It is not only having the book but also being able to read it that gives power to the owner. In the Middle Ages only the clergy could read; thus it was the Church that had the greatest power during that time. With the invention of the printing press, books became available to the masses and knowledge spread. However, not all of us assign as much importance to knowledge as we should. Thus even today, it is the people who are in the know, who are privy to private knowledge, who hold the most power. The BOOK picture tells you to be aware of the paths of communication around you and advises you to use them to your advantage. The period of influence is short, as knowledge and news are ever changing.

POSITION 1: Someone will communicate a secret to you. This can be a secret at work, or simply a friend telling you about a secret activity. The secret will give you a better understanding of the situation and benefit you as you will know how to act accordingly. For people who want to advance in their jobs, it is important to attend meetings, read bulletins, update skills, and have friendly luncheons with fellow workers. In this way you can gather knowledge about the company; know where it is going and who is going to make it work. You are not using people if you are open with them and share your ideas as well as hear their ideas. It is wise not to disclose the secret you have heard or to use it for any illegal purpose.

POSITION 2: Someone is hiding information that is important to you. It doesn't have to be done maliciously; it can simply be that the person doesn't think the information concerns you. When you get this picture, be supersensitive to the information that is flowing around you. Keep your ears open so that what people are communicating, you will receive. If changes are occurring at your work place, home, or recreational center, it is a good idea to be aware of them so that you can put in for the best deal possible for you and not be handed what is left over. In any personal relationship, it is also a good idea to examine what the other person might be hiding from you. This is especially important for people contemplating marriage. A friend of mine was totally smitten by a charming, loving, thoughtful man who had entered her life. It was only after she married him that she discovered he kept his vodka bottles in the clothes hamper. Had she been more careful and observant in the first place, she would have avoided a lot of pain and grief.

POSITION 3: The secret you have been told is going to be disclosed. Either you or someone else will make it public. Knowledge and information are ever changing and what is secret one minute can be public the next. This should be of no concern to you if you have been aboveboard and honest in your dealings. This is why it is not a good idea to try to use secret knowledge for illegal purposes; you will be found out. You might feel hurt or resentful when a private or intimate secret is disclosed. However, that is life, always changing. Your confidant may still be your good friend, but circumstances have changed and made the disclosure necessary. The Russians say: You can't hide an awl in a cloth bag. In other words, you can't hide secrets; someone always finds out.

POSITION 4: Your talkativeness will bring you harm. For example, a defendant may lose the case not because he is wrong, but because he doesn't know when he has presented the relevant facts and continues with immaterial details that confuse the jury. People can have good arguments, but when they go on and on, the listener gets bored and tunes out. It is sad to see some people who seem to be so starved for company that when they are with friends, all they do is talk incessantly about such trivial matters that all their friends want to do is escape their company. An attractive man or woman can easily dispel the illusion of attractiveness by opening his or her mouth and chattering about unimportant and uninteresting things. The Russian proverb forewarns: The stupid are discovered by their words.

When you get this picture, stop and listen to yourself. Are you really contributing to the conversation or just letting your vocal chords run wild? Are you disclosing information that was confided to you and will hurt or embarrass another person? Are you letting out your ideas prematurely, so that they can be used by another before you are ready to use them yourself? Many people have been deterred from success by talking prematurely about their ideas and meeting negative responses. Remember, we were given two ears and one mouth, so do twice as much listening as talking.

27 LETTER

PERIOD OF INFLUENCE: immediate to short

SYMBOL FOR: news from a distance

MEANING: ↓ 1. Happiness will come to you from far away.
  → 2. Interesting, unexpected news.
  ← 3. You will hear a long-awaited word.
  ↑ 4. Sad news.

GENERAL MEANING OF PICTURE: Ever since humans learned to write and read, the letter has been a means of spreading information and delivering news. Thus the LETTER picture indicates some type of news. Its period of influence is immediate and of short duration, as news becomes old very fast.

POSITION 1: Happiness will come to you from far away. It could come by letter or by other more modern means such as telephone, telex, computer, or fax machine. The news could be something that will affect your life and make you happy, like your proposal or request for something being accepted. On the other hand, the news could be regarding someone else who is close to you. Something good has happened in this person's life, and you are happy knowing this.

POSITION 2: You will hear interesting, unexpected news. This can be news of any kind. It will be good news, but something totally unexpected.

POSITION 3: You will hear a long-awaited word. This again could be anything that you have been waiting to hear. If you have been waiting for a marriage proposal, then now is a likely time to get it. If you have been waiting for a raise or a promotion, then you will hear it now. Generally, you don't have to seek the information now, as it will come of its own accord.

The picture may refer to getting a letter or news from someone who is far away and hasn't written for a while. You have been thinking about this person. Finally you will hear from or about him or her.

POSITION 4: You will hear sad news. This news can be regarding your own interests or relating to someone you know well.

28 HORSESHOE

PERIOD OF INFLUENCE: middle

SYMBOL FOR: success

MEANING: ↓ 1. Good fortune awaits you.
→ 2. Everything that you undertake in the near future will be successful.
← 3. Your desire will be fulfilled.
↑ 4. You will walk by happiness not noticing it.

GENERAL MEANING OF PICTURE: Like the CLOVER picture, the HORSESHOE picture tells of great luck or success. However, the CLOVER implies pure luck by chance, while the HORSESHOE implies luck or good fortune due to one's efforts. Humans were able to use the first domesticated animal, the horse, better by inventing the horseshoe. Thus our efforts at inventing, pursuing, or working very hard at something will bring us good fortune.

POSITION 1: Good fortune or great success awaits you. If during the reading you asked how a certain idea or proposal of yours will do and you get this picture in this position, you know that you will meet with success. This could be a job you are applying for, a promotion you've been pushing for, a bid to purchase something, a thesis submission, or an idea that you want to pursue. The signal is a green light: go ahead with your plans, as they will meet with approval and be successful. The period of influence is of middle duration, which means the effects will last anywhere from a few days to a few years. You will be successful, but only to the degree that you put effort into it. Don't just sit back and wish for success; do something to get it.

The picture tells you that your ideas and efforts are worthwhile and will meet with great success if you pursue them. Don't be afraid of ideas that seem different or innovative. The Russians joke by saying: You're not like your mother or father, but like the handsome passer-by. You have talents that make you different from your family. Use your talents and great success will follow.

POSITION 2: Everything that you undertake in the near future will be successful. This can refer to important projects, and it can also refer to everyday happenings. Any projects you undertake at work will be successful. When you get this picture it can be a good time to try out new ideas or methods of doing something that you have been considering, as you will meet with success at this time. This is also an opportune time to start a diet, an exercise program, or any self-improvement program you have been thinking about. It is always a pleasure to get this picture, as it tells you that life will flow smoothly for a while, with everything turning out well. As mentioned earlier, it could simply mean that everyday activities will all be successful. You will feel invincible, able to do and face anything.

POSITION 3: Your desire will be fulfilled. Whatever you have been wishing for will come true. This can be a material thing like getting the expensive coat or the car that you have been dreaming of, or it can be achieving a goal that you have been striving for. Generally, it is something that you have been working on or dreaming of for some time. It is a good idea to let other people know some of your wishes, so that they can also assist in making them happen. It is better to let others know what you desire than to silently wait for them to find out and then be disappointed in not getting what you really wanted. However, this should not be carried to an extreme, as it can make you too demanding and can limit your experiences. The idea is to make sure that you set goals and have dreams that can come true. No wish or idea is too farfetched to happen; it is only you who sets limits on how far you can go.

POSITION 4: You will walk by happiness without noticing it. This is a contradiction in terms, for how do you know it is happiness if you don't see it? It is easier to notice other people doing this than to realize you are doing it yourself. For example, a friend of mine has two children. The oldest is a boy and gets most of his parents' attention. The second, a daughter, is probably brighter and more talented, yet she does not get the same attention from the parents. You can see the look of disappointment on her face often, yet the parents don't notice it. They don't do it out of meanness; rather, it is a blind spot they have that they are not even aware of. We all have such blind spots, and the picture reminds us of this.

Perhaps you are more task-oriented than people-oriented. Later in life you might regret not having spent more time with your children or parents, instead of having squandered it on keeping the cleanest house on the block. When you get this picture, look carefully around you and try to notice what you are perhaps not seeing. Listen to friends; they could be telling you what you don't see. You might not like what people are telling you and want to reject it, but maybe you should listen, as your present or future happiness could depend on it. Another friend of mine related the story of a young man who stayed with them. He was a top national athlete, a straight-A student, handsome, charming, funny, and generally a pleasure to be with. He told them that his father had abandoned him and his mother at his birth. How sad for the father, to have walked away from what most people desire.

29 MONEY

PERIOD OF INFLUENCE: middle

SYMBOL FOR: money

MEANING: ↓ 1. You will receive a substantial sum of money.
        → 2. You will find success or profit in an undertaking.
        ← 3. An unexpected pleasant windfall.
        ↑ 4. A long wait before receiving earned money.

GENERAL MEANING OF PICTURE: The money picture is self-explanatory—it deals with money. The picture foretells of money that will be received, or it can indicate a favorable time for monetary gain. The nice aspect of the picture is that it indicates money to be received in every position. Material loss is shown by the SHIP picture in position 4.

The MONEY picture refers to legitimate, legal ways of making money. It also applies when you are speculating or betting in legal ways. The picture only tells you that it is a favorable time to make money; it does not guarantee that you will make money every time. Should the cards be used to determine timing for illegal activities, they will not give you the right answer.

POSITION 1: You will receive a substantial sum of money. This picture usually appears just before you receive an income-tax refund, a larger than usual paycheck, a bonus, a commission, or interest. Usually you are aware that you will be getting a large sum; nevertheless, it is still a pleasant surprise when you get it.

If you are entering negotiations of any kind, then the picture tells you that you will come out with a good settlement.

106

POSITION 2: You will find success or profit in an undertaking. Your efforts are going to be rewarded. This is a good time to conclude any financial business that you have. It is also a good time to buy things that will appreciate in value, such as houses, furniture, antiques, some jewelry, or anything that you think is a good buy.

You should also check any old stocks or bonds that you may have forgotten. Now is a good time to cash them in. Remember, bonds expire after a certain date and stop earning interest. Make sure you check the dates, to maximize your profits.

If you are beginning a new business venture and this picture comes up, then you know that the business will be a financial success.

POSITION 3: An unexpected pleasant windfall. You will gain money, but not as much as indicated by the picture in the first two positions. This could mean receiving something for free that you would generally have to pay for yourself—for example, a free ticket to a football game or a concert.

The picture may also refer to unexpected labor that you are asked to perform. It might be something that is your hobby, or something that you simply enjoy doing. All of a sudden someone is willing to pay you for what you enjoy doing anyway. A friend may ask you to be a photographer at her wedding, or you might be asked to be a security guard at a favorite rock group's concert. You will not earn a fortune from these ventures, but you will have a good time.

POSITION 4: A long wait before receiving earned money. This may seem like a disappointment, yet the money will come. If you are self-employed, you know that it will be a while before you receive payment. Students who work in the summer sometimes have to wait a month or two before receiving their total wages.

If you have purchased stocks hoping to make a quick profit and this picture comes up, then you know that your immediate plans will not turn out. Two years ago, on the advice of my son, I bought some gold shares that were supposed to double in value overnight. After a week when nothing happened, I did a reading and the MONEY picture appeared in this position. I knew then that I would eventually make money on the stocks and that I should not despair even though the shares had fallen to half their original value. A year later, the stocks went up and I made a small profit. The advice here is not to despair or get panicky, but to patiently wait the situation out.

30 LILY

PERIOD OF INFLUENCE: life

SYMBOL FOR: faithfulness

MEANING: ↓ 1. A happy life full of meaning.
       → 2. You will know in life faithfulness till death.
       ← 3. Unearthly happiness.
       ↑ 4. Useless doubts about faithfulness; jealousy.

GENERAL MEANING OF PICTURE: The LILY is another life picture that symbolizes beauty, purity, love, faithfulness, and caring. The lily at Easter stands for death and rebirth. It is a tall, regal, and beautiful flower. Its fragrance is sweet and enduring. The lily is like Christ's life, noble yet gentle and pure. Because it is pure white and has such a heavenly smell, we associate it with heavenly or spiritual powers. The BOUQUET refers to earthly, physical happiness, while the LILY refers to spiritual happiness.

POSITION 1: You will have a happy life full of meaning. This picture applies to your entire life. You will not get it every time; it usually appears at times when you have doubts or problems. It is a reminder to be true to yourself, to follow your gut reactions, as they are valid and will bring you to a successful outcome. The picture tells you that you will have a happy life. This does not mean that you will have no problems or sad periods, but rather that overall your life will be more happy than sad. It also tells you that your life will be full of meaning. This means that the field of work you have chosen will benefit the world or humankind in some way. Christ's life is the ultimate example of a happy life that was full of meaning. His teachings of loving each other and caring for the poor have endured for two thousand years. Your efforts don't have to be so grand. Yet whatever you do will be of benefit to others, as well as make you happy.

POSITION 2: You will know in life faithfulness till your death. The picture speaks of more than just love; it means the total caring, loving, and sharing of joy found in a good relationship. The Russians say: You can measure the depth of the sea but not the depth of the heart. You are indeed lucky to have found such a fathomless love in our present busy world. The picture does not necessarily have to relate to faithfulness between a man and a woman, but can refer to any relationship that is nurturing to you and makes your life better.

POSITION 3: You will experience unearthly happiness. This means the happiness is more than being happy over some material gain; it is the pure joy of just being alive, of being a part of this wonderful universe. This feeling can be triggered by some accomplishment by you or someone in your family or work place. Perhaps you have gotten a promotion, or your daughter has just won a scholarship, or you have just finished weeding your raspberry patch. Whatever the reason, you will have an almost spiritual feeling of happiness. Of course, the picture can also refer to spiritual happiness, the feeling of being one with God.

POSITION 4: Useless doubts about faithfulness; jealousy. This is a very reassuring picture for those who suspect that their spouses are having an affair. The SNAKE picture in position 2 will warn you of unfaithfulness, while the LILY picture reassures you that your jealousy is for nothing. Even if your spouse is out with someone of the opposite sex, their conversation and actions are such that you don't have to worry, as your love relationship will not be affected. The reliability of this picture has been tested many times; the picture has spared people many hours of anguish. Jealousy is called the green-eyed monster for the havoc it can cause for those involved, but mainly for the person who is jealous. If you can spare yourself the tormenting fits of jealousy by taking to heart the reassurance of this picture, then you can add years of happiness and peace to your life.

31 SUN

PERIOD OF INFLUENCE: immediate to middle

SYMBOL FOR: warmth and strength of character

MEANING: ↓ 1. Prosperity, flourishment, life's caress, happiness.
→ 2. Warmth and light are within you alone.
← 3. A lack of courage hinders you from obtaining your wish.
↑ 4. Coldness of the heart will freeze you.

GENERAL MEANING OF PICTURE: The sun is the center of our solar system. It radiates the heat and light that make life possible on earth. From earliest times, humans have worshiped the sun as the giver of life. The sun was the main object of worship for both the Aztecs and the Egyptians, who believed that humankind is the descendant of the sun god. In Eastern cultures it is the yang, the force that brings warmth and flourishment and keeps evil away. Thus not only are we affected by the physical sun that we see in the sky, but the sun is the self as well, the inner flame that burns within us and gives us life. We are the center of our social and physical environments. What we radiate from within affects the lives of the people around us. We are the sun that the picture refers to. When we radiate warmth from within, we are happy and have a positive influence on the people around us. When we freeze up, we push people away from us, causing unhappiness to everyone, including ourselves.

POSITION 1: This is one of the nicest pictures to get in this position. It means that you are at your best. Prosperity, flourishment, life's caress, and happiness are all yours. You are in a wonderful phase; you are warm, beautiful or handsome, understanding, and as such, attract positive vibrations and people to you. It means that you are happy with yourself and therefore use your positive energy in a constructive way in whatever you are doing. You radiate health and vitality and people are impressed with your energy. Because you are happy, you have the time and energy to look at others and make them feel good as well. This is the time when you are smiling at the world and the world is smiling back at you.

This also can be a time to take courses or learn a new skill—anything that will develop you further as a worthwhile being. If the picture comes up when you are having difficulties, it is telling you to trust yourself. By working on your positive qualities, you will master the situation.

POSITION 2: You are the master of your life; warmth and light are within you alone. No one but you, will help or hurt you. Don't look for someone else to make you happy or love you. Begin by loving yourself. Do things that make you happy. Others will inevitably be drawn to you.

This picture comes up quite often when people are in difficulty and need help. The picture tells you that it is no use seeking help from others, as they can't help you or simply don't want to. The truth is that you don't need anyone else's help, as you are capable of solving your own problems. For example, the picture may come up for you during difficult times in your marriage. When it comes up, you should know that it is not the time to talk to your partner, as nothing will get resolved. Rather, it is a time to work on improving yourself as an individual, by finishing your education, getting a job, cutting your hair, losing weight, or simply going out and doing things that make you happy. Ironically enough, once you are happy with yourself and self-confident, your relationship problems will iron themselves out.

The picture also can come up when your family or the group you are with is in difficulty. At that time it is you who has the energy and radiance that gives the other people support. You don't have to do anything for them, only stay positive and friendly; this is enough to pull them through their difficulties.

POSITION 3: A lack of courage prevents you from getting what you want. Just the acknowledgment of this fact can put a person at ease.

Look at your life and note where you are stagnant. What do you want but lack the courage to get? The picture can refer to major things like getting a raise at work or to minor things like asking your neighbor not to cut the grass on Sunday morning. Once you have isolated what you want, then you can begin to work on the problem. If you really want it, then you should pursue it when this picture comes up. This is the SUN picture, telling you that you have the capability to obtain what you desire.

If you lack the courage to personally ask for or seek what you want, you can look for alternate ways of achieving it. If you are afraid to ask directly, perhaps you can write a letter or think of an imaginative way of presenting your case. You also can ask other people to help you. They can do the courageous act while you repay them in other ways.

The thing to remember is that we don't have to be courageous in all circumstances. There are many different types of courage, and what one sees as courageous can be viewed by another as dangerous or foolish. My friend laughs at me because I am afraid of heights and won't go mountain climbing or cross perilous precipices. I could brace myself to do it, but it isn't important for me to be courageous in this situation. Talking in front of people also takes a lot of courage. I would rather save my energy for public speaking, which I enjoy, than waste it on something I get little pleasure out of.

Do not let the lack of courage prevent .you from getting the important things in your life. For example, a beginning teacher spent ten minutes sitting in the washroom before class, gathering courage to face the students. The teacher was terrified, yet by conquering her fear, she was able to begin a new career. Should you get this picture in this position and you lack the courage to do something that is really important to your future, do go ahead, no matter how scared you are. You will meet with success.

POSITION 4: You will be frozen by a coldness of the heart. This is a state when you feel neither pain nor love, just emptiness. It usually follows intense emotional experiences. You have given more than your share, till finally you are worn out, finished. This neutral state is only temporary. It is a time to quietly concentrate on your affairs and avoid dealing with people, as you will not show the positive aspects of your personality. Have a smile on your face, no matter how cold or withdrawn you might feel at the time, and don't get into any arguments or heavy discussions. Realize that aloofness and indifference are also powerful emotions and can accomplish much in certain circumstances, where friendliness has not succeeded.

32 MOON

PERIOD OF INFLUENCE: short to middle

SYMBOL FOR: peace

MEANING: ↓ 1. Although your life is uneventful, you have happiness nevertheless.
→ 2. If you are patient, you will obtain that which you desire.
← 3. Do not become despondent over a temporary setback.
↑ 4. Delay in action will work against you.

GENERAL MEANING OF PICTURE: The moon, like the sun, has been worshiped by many cultures. The sun is the overt radiator of energy, while the moon is the covert, hidden reflector of energy. The sun is the yang, the male force, while the moon is the yin, the female force. The moon affects us by its peace, beauty, and mystery. We are just as much attracted to calm, serene, and graceful people as we are to the radiant, full-of-energy types who represent the sun. Like the earth, which needs both the heat of the sun and the coolness of the moon to maintain life, so we need both aspects of ourselves to stay balanced. There are times when we need to act, and there are times when we need to be calm and reflect on life. Our Western culture places a great amount of value on activity, which when carried too far results in burnout and dissatisfaction. That is why many have been turning to the Eastern culture, to meditation and yoga, to provide the peace that is lacking in our modern urban environment. However, too much inactivity can also lead to unhappiness and misery, as seen in some parts of Asia. Thus, we have to learn to balance both sides of our nature. The MOON picture is always a reminder to us to appreciate the calm periods in our lives. The moon changes from full to half to quarter, so that the calmness is not static, but ever changing. When we get this picture, it is a time to relax, but not to abandon our dreams.

POSITION 1: Although your life is uneventful, you have happiness nevertheless. The picture tells you to smell the roses; enjoy the life that you are leading at the moment, because it is happiness. We are constantly inundated with information about the lives of the rich and famous, and our own surroundings pale in comparison. However, there is more to happiness than fancy clothes and cars. Nature, family, satisfying work, love, and health are all things that make for happiness. When this picture comes up, take a closer look at what you have and enjoy it to the utmost. Peace doesn't last forever, so take the time to relish it while it is here. The Russian proverb reminds you: What we have we don't treasure; having lost it we cry. Don't waste your time wishing for things you don't have; rather, enjoy your peaceful happiness.

POSITION 2: If you are patient, you will attain that which you desire. This is hard for some people to do, to relax in the heat of battle. Still, even the best soldier needs to bide his time between battles. Sometimes you need to wait and let others do things or come to conclusions on their own that will be of benefit to you in the end. Also, many of your wishes take longer to accomplish than you think. The picture tells you to relax, be patient, and keep on working toward your desires, as ultimately you will accomplish them.

POSITION 3: Don't become despondent over a temporary setback. One of the saddest things in life is to see people struggle to accomplish a goal and then almost at the end, give up due to some problem. Students sometimes struggle for nine months and then at the end skip school, don't finish their assignments, or miss the final test. Had they hung in just a bit longer, they would have passed through sheer perseverance and not just by grades. Even famous people such as Benjamin Franklin, Winston Churchill, and Colonel Sanders had many setbacks in their lives before they achieved their success. This picture has appeared for me many times during the writing of this book. The power of the picture is that it tells you that your goal is a

116

valid one and can be attained even though you might have rejections at the present time. There are other pictures, such as the OWL, SHIP, and HOUSE, that tell you your plans or ideas may not materialize or be accomplished. When the MOON picture comes up, don't give up your efforts. Like the ebb and tide of the oceans caused by the pull of the moon, you will have glorious successes and glorious disappointments along the way, but the energy never ceases.

POSITION 4: Delay in action will work against you. He who hesitates is lost, or as the Russians say it: The turkey thought and thought, then expired. This is not the time to contemplate matters; rather, it is the time for making decisions and putting them into action. The moon is never constant as it goes through its phases. In position 4, it is a full moon, which resembles the sun and signifies that action is needed on your part. Sitting back and letting the world unfold will not work in your favor at this time. You have to initiate the action if you want something done. If you want a raise, companionship, or excitement, then it is up to you. Because this is the MOON picture, the best action is subtle, peaceful but determined. State your wishes clearly, precisely, and in a graceful manner for best results. If you are doing an activity, then do it smoothly with as little friction as possible for best results.

33 FISH

PERIOD OF INFLUENCE: short to middle

SYMBOL FOR: material and/or spiritual fortune

MEANING: ↓ 1. Fortune, especially on the sea.
→ 2. If you want success, seek it on the water and not on land.
← 3. Trade will bring profit.
↑ 4. In a difficult moment you won't sink but will rise to the surface.

GENERAL MEANING OF PICTURE: The FISH picture has a dual meaning. On the first level, it stands for plenty, abundance of food. On the second level, the fish symbolizes spiritual life. The picture can be interpreted either way or synergistically.

As a picture of plenty, the FISH symbolizes the material needs that people have. Fish used to be plentiful in the oceans and seas. If you could find a means of catching the fish, you were guaranteed to make a fortune.

On the second level, the fish symbolizes spiritual life. Early Christians used the fish as a symbol to identify themselves. Christ used a few fish to feed thousands of people. After crucifixion, Christ appeared to the fishermen and told them to go forth and spread his word to the world. He divided one loaf of bread to feed all of them. He showed them that their physical needs would be met as long as they grew spiritually. Similarly in the Buddhist religion, monks who are pursuing spiritual goals are fed by the population at large. The spiritual meaning of the picture is not confined to any particular

118

religion; rather, it refers to the universal God. The picture tells you to listen to your inner spiritual feelings which will guide you to your destination.

The FISH can also refer to a synergistic combination of the physical and the spiritual. The proverb "Man does not live by bread alone" says the same thing. For us to be truly happy, we must take care of both our physical and spiritual needs. The picture is a reminder to some that they should be taking care of their spiritual needs at this time.

POSITION 1: Fortune, especially on the sea. As mentioned earlier, the picture can have two meanings. On the first level, seek fortune on the seas. Anything to do with the seas—fishing, scuba diving, oceanography, cruise ships—will lead you to success. You will either make money or meet someone who will complete your life.

On the second level, the picture tells you to seek your fortune in spiritual matters. Material things will not bring you happiness at this time. Even other people will not fulfill the need that you have. This is the time to get in touch with yourself and do something that interests you or is unique to you. If you can contribute to make the world a better place, you will also make yourself happy at the same time. Write the book you have always wanted to write, compose songs, become a Big Brother or Big Sister, read to the blind, join a religious organization, or go to a foreign country and work with the poor. Each person has a unique talent or personality trait that can help humankind.

When the picture appears in this position, whatever you have undertaken will flow easily. You have a chance at making a great contribution to the world. Fortune awaits you, not necessarily in the monetary sense but in the self-satisfaction that you get from knowing that you have done your best.

During the many years I spent writing this book, whenever the picture appeared in this position, the writing was very easy for me. It was as though someone were guiding my fingers.

POSITION 2: If you want success, seek it on the water and not on land. This is similar to the picture in position 1, but less forceful. In position 1 it indicates that you can make a great contribution to humankind, while in position 2 it speaks of lesser, more personal goals. Again the double meaning. Anything to do with water will bring success. This can be water of any kind, from drinking water to rain clouds to snowmobiles and ice breakers. If you are looking for a job, then look into any area that has something to do with water. If you are looking for a place to live, then somewhere near water will bring success to you.

On the second level, seek success in nonmaterialistic ways. Meditation, prayer, and creative visualization are some of the techniques that may help you at this time. These techniques relieve stress and give you peace of mind. Once rested, you can proceed to everyday matters with a much clearer head and a rested body.

This picture has come up for people who have seemed unlikely to have the sensitivity to seek a spiritual life. On second consideration, these are the very ones who need to get in touch with their spiritual selves. The purely physical existence they are leading isn't making them happy. A number of years ago, a friend's neighbor had a reading done. He was about fifty, a carpenter, married and with grown children. Physically he had everything he wanted. Yet he was so unhappy that his wife was on the verge of leaving him. The picture came up for him in this position. All of a sudden he began talking about ideas he had that had been dormant. I don't know what happened to him, but I hope that he pursued those seeds of spiritual awakening.

POSITION 3: Trade will bring profit. Don't sell yourself short. Whatever you have, whether it be a material good or a talent, is worthy and should not be undervalued. People respect those who know their value. If you are looking into buying or selling something, then don't take the first offer. Trading or bargaining will bring you a profit. If you are looking for a job, then anything to do with commerce will be good for you. If you are working already but not getting very far as the long hours are not producing the income that you would like, then you should reevaluate your position. This is a good time to ask for a raise. Or perhaps you should let go of a job that does not pay well and seek a better-paying job. This is a good time to undertake anything that will improve your financial status.

POSITION 4: In a difficult moment you will not sink but will rise to the surface. No matter what blow life may deal you, you will be able to handle it. This picture appears when people feel down, disappointed, or abandoned. The picture is always a support, an uplifting force. It tells you that you have the courage and inner resources to rise above any problems. Your best character traits will come to the surface and will help you out of your difficulty. If it is finding a job, getting over a broken marriage or love affair, or recovering from anything that has you down, you will be able to master the situation. Remember David and Goliath. David, even with all the odds against him, was able to slay Goliath.

If your troubles seem so insurmountable that suicide seems the only way out, *don't do it*. It is not only your inner strength that makes you rise to the surface. Like the water currents that help a fish rise to the surface, so heavenly powers will assist you in surmounting your problems.

34 OWL

PERIOD OF INFLUENCE: short

SYMBOL FOR: problems with immediate projects

MEANING: ↓ 1. At the present time you want to act unwisely.
→ 2. Your cunning schemes will be exposed.
← 3. Your project will be unsuccessful.
↑ 4. Your plans will not materialize.

GENERAL MEANING OF PICTURE: In Western society, the owl has stood for wisdom. This is probably because the owl doesn't seem to waste energy. It looks like it is thinking or observing a situation very carefully before attacking its prey. In Eastern cultures, the owl is looked at in a more negative way—too much yin, almost like a ghost—although not as evil. Both interpretations are suited to the OWL picture. Generally, the card refers to projects we have undertaken. These are usually vital to our existence, just as the prey is vital to the owl's existence. In every position, the picture tells us to look carefully at our projects, as there seem to be some problems with them.

POSITION 1: At the present moment you want to act unwisely. Perhaps you want to invest money when you shouldn't, or pursue a losing proposition, or even give up on a plan that you should continue. Whatever project you are involved with at work or at home needs to be examined carefully. You should be like the owl; sit back quietly and ponder the situation. What is the best action to take at this time? Remember that this picture relates only to the next week or weeks, and what you put off today can be picked up again in a week or

122

two. The picture also can refer to family matters, relationships with family members. In this case, think twice before you do anything definite. Or follow the Russian adage: Measure seven times, cut once. It doesn't hurt to go slowly at this time.

POSITION 2: Your cunning actions or schemes will be exposed. You only need to worry if what you have been doing is underhanded or illegal. Most of us do plan projects that we are afraid to talk about because people might laugh at us or talk us out of our plans. These plans need to be kept personal till the right time. The OWL picture can refer to these plans, telling you that it is time to make public your plans. The picture indicates that there is an element of cunning to your plans. Are you doing something that is underhanded? Are you doing something that might hurt someone else or simply something to protect yourself? Sometimes at work there are people who are self-centered. Unless we look after our own interests we are left with all the unwanted chores and jobs. Since the picture tells you that your slyness will be exposed, make sure that you do not appear in a bad light. As long as you haven't done anything intentionally to hurt someone else, you don't need to be overly apologetic or act guilty. Sometimes by exposing the scheme yourself, you take the sting out of it. Just remember that everything you do can come to light, so make sure you are honest in all your covert actions.

POSITION 3: Your project will be unsuccessful. This is usually a project that is already under way. It could be a job interview, a paper you are writing, a car you are fixing, or anything that you are working on. Again, stop and think. Give yourself some time to reassess the project. Perhaps it is not a total loss, but needs a different perspective. Or it could be that it is not worth pursuing. In either case, be like the wise owl by giving yourself time to ponder the situation. You don't have to catch every mouse; another one will come along that might be even a better catch.

POSITION 4: Your desired plans will not materialize. These are plans that you want but have not yet begun to put into action. The plans could relate to a vacation or a trip you are thinking of, an idea you want to put into action, or a change you want to make in yourself or your environment. If you are asking the cards whether to proceed with your desired plans and this picture comes up, then you know that the answer is no. This is not the time to spend your energy on this plan, as it will fail at this time.

35 ANCHOR

PERIOD OF INFLUENCE: middle

SYMBOL FOR: stability or hindrance

MEANING: ↓ 1. Success in love; you are loved.
         → 2. Fulfillment of hopes; success on the sea.
         ← 3. Disillusionment with the ideal; doubts.
         ↑ 4. Your mistake will be difficult to correct.

GENERAL MEANING OF PICTURE: The anchor refers to stability. Sailors use the anchor to secure their boats once they have reached a safe harbor. In the first two positions, the picture tells you that you have reached a safe haven in your life. Your love relationships, home, or work are safe, giving you protection and stability. Anchors can also be a hindrance, preventing movement. In the last two positions, this picture suggests you may have doubts or have actually chosen a wrong place to anchor.

POSITION 1: You have success in love; you are loved. This is a true love, one that makes you feel safe and comfortable. This card usually refers to romantic love, but it can also refer to anyone else who provides a loving haven for you. All too often people seek romantic love and ignore the real love that is around them because it doesn't fit their preconceived image. When this picture comes up, look around you to see who is offering love to you. By being loving yourself you can fully enjoy the safe haven the anchor provides.

POSITION 2: Fulfillment of hopes; success on the sea. Perhaps you have already or are about to receive what you have been hoping for. After sailing on the open sea, you are approaching your destination.

This could be having the family you want, the house of your dreams, the job you have wanted, or anything you have been working toward. Success on the sea can literally mean that your good fortune has something to do with the sea, or it can mean that whatever you are involved with you should pursue full steam ahead as it will turn out successfully.

POSITION 3: Disillusionment with the ideal; doubts. You don't know if you have chosen the right place to put your anchor down. This card often comes up if you have problems with a situation or have reached an impasse in your life. For example, you could be disappointed with the relationship you are having with the person you love and begin to wonder if the person is the right one for you. Or you could be disappointed with your children because they are not behaving the way you want them to; you begin to doubt yourself as a good parent. We also have doubts many times in our lives relating to the job or occupation that we have chosen. Did we make the right decision or are we wasting our time? The important thing to remember when you get this picture is that it doesn't tell you that you have done something wrong, only that you are disappointed that it isn't the way you envisioned it to be. It is a time to reexamine your priorities, to look at your life from all angles, to see if you have made some mistakes that have led you to this disillusioned period. Have you put down your anchor prematurely or in the wrong place? This is not a time to wallow in self-pity, but to do some constructive thinking. It is a time to pull up the anchor and begin solving the problem in a new, creative way. The disillusionment will not last forever unless you let it.

POSITION 4: Your mistake will be difficult to correct. Here the picture tells you that you have made a mistake or used poor judgment. You have put down your anchor in the wrong place. You will probably suffer some loss or disappointment. Having made a mistake, admit it to yourself or anyone else involved, take the loss, and go on with your life. If you want to correct your mistake, you can, but it will be difficult to do so. Sometimes by admitting we were wrong, we are already correcting the mistake.

36   HANDSHAKE

PERIOD OF INFLUENCE: middle to life

SYMBOL FOR: state of the union between two people

MEANING: ↓ 1. A strong friendship will be a support to you for your entire life.
→ 2. Love will weld you into one with the person you love.
← 3. The handshake will weaken if you don't make the effort to strengthen it.
↑ 4. Your union threatens to come apart.

GENERAL MEANING OF PICTURE: The handshake has usually signified an agreement between two people, whether for friendly or business reasons. The picture quite often refers to the state of marriage or union that you have. The BRANCHES and RING pictures also pertain to the union but have slightly different meanings. When the HANDSHAKE picture comes up in the first two positions, you know that your relationship with a loved person is on solid ground. You are more than lovers, you are also friends. In the last two positions, the picture warns you of a weakening of the union. The picture also can refer to a business deal, especially if the deal depends upon the partners' being good friends. The meaning in this case is similar to that given for a romantic union between people, except that the words *business deal* should replace the words *union* or *relationship*.

POSITION 1: A strong friendship will be a support to you for your entire life. This usually is the friendship of the person you are living with or are involved with in a strong way. In contrast, the DOG

127

picture refers to being strictly friends, even lifelong friends. If you are jealous or worried about your relationship and this picture comes up, then you know your worries are unnecessary. The picture also shows up when you are having other problems. It gives you reassurance that you have someone to rely on, no matter what problems you might be having. It is a life picture, meaning that the relationship is a lasting one.

POSITION 2: Love will weld you into one with the person you love. This can be a new romance, or a new strong feeling toward the person you are involved with. In either case, the love you have is a good one, based on respect. This bond or welding into one doesn't necessarily occur at the time of marriage, when you are passionately in love, but can occur later when you get to know the person better and truly begin to appreciate her or him.

POSITION 3: The handshake will weaken if you don't make an effort to strengthen it. This is a sound warning, telling you that your union is in danger. You should devote more time to the other person or to the relationship. Quite often we get so carried away with our jobs, activities, or children that we forget to put the same amount of energy into our closest relationship. Or we get bored with the other person or the relationship and think we are justified in seeking other stimulants. If the picture comes up in this position, then it is a time for you to take a closer look at your relationship. Do you want to continue it? And if so, what can you do to strengthen the bond? The picture warns you that it is up to you to make the effort to strengthen the relationship. It is you and not the other person who is at fault. Remember that spouses don't usually stray from a healthy, vital relationship. Look into the past and try to remember what brought the two of you together in the first place. Then do whatever pleases the other person, to rekindle the old romantic spark. Or cut down on the outside activities with which you are involved in order to devote more time to the relationship. In either case you'll be a winner because you will regain a strong relationship, which is the main support you have in life.

POSITION 4: Your union is definitely in trouble and threatens to come apart. This is a much stronger warning than that given by the picture in position 3. Here both parties could be at fault. If you are jealous and suspect that the other person is having an affair and this picture comes up, then your suspicions could be justified, especially if the SNAKE picture comes up in position 2 as well. However, nothing is final. If after examining the situation carefully you decide that you want to continue your relationship, then you should do everything in your power to preserve it. The picture usually comes up at times in your life when a breakup is possible but not necessarily inevitable. Look at the advice given in position 3 and follow it as well. If you can overcome your difficulties, find new solutions, then you will end up on a higher plateau, reach a deeper understanding between the two of you. Even infidelity can be forgiven and forgotten, as long as you have established or reestablished a strong union.

37 ANGEL

PERIOD OF INFLUENCE: middle

SYMBOL FOR: guardian angel helping you

MEANING: ↓ 1. A bright, wished-for happiness awaits you.
→ 2. Reconciliation will give you joy.
← 3. Love and tenderness will comfort you.
↑ 4. Heavenly powers will save you from a false step.

GENERAL MEANING OF PICTURE: The ANGEL is my favorite picture. When you get it, it is as though your life lights up like a light bulb.

The angel may be our guardian angel that prevents us from false actions and urges us to do good deeds. The angel does not have to be connected to Christian beliefs; it is a universal spirit of goodness and protection. It is a feeling that one is not alone, that there is a universal power greater than oneself. The power is with us, guiding us to do the best we can. The power also helps us choose the correct path in life.

In all four positions, the picture tells you that you are not alone. You are on the correct path. The universal goodness, or angel, or soul, will protect you.

POSITION 1: A bright, desired happiness or good fortune awaits you. You will have success in whatever you are pursuing. This can be the joy of triumph or the attainment of a goal you have been working toward. You will finally quit smoking, run your first marathon, discover a cure for AIDS, get a promotion at work, or the like. It can also mean simple joy, like attaining the family happiness you have wanted. Generally, the happiness is of the spirit rather than derived from possession of material goods. The important thing is to enjoy the good fortune while you have it; celebrate your success.

POSITION 2: Reconciliation will give you joy. The usual reconciliation is between husband and wife, parents and children, or close friends. The relationship is quite close, either with family or people you love. If you are having problems communicating, then the picture tells you that this is a good time to make an effort at reestablishing contact. The other person will be responsive. Great joy will come to both of you from the effort. It is as though heavenly powers want you to reconcile at this time.

The picture can also refer to reconciliation with oneself, accepting some aspect of your life that you can't change. Accepting some physical handicap or separation from loved ones can lead to a positive end, while feelings of anger, despair, or regret simply sap your energies. It is the reconciliation, overcoming your troubles, that gives you a feeling of joy.

POSITION 3: Love and tenderness will comfort you. The picture reminds you that you are loved even though you may be experiencing problems in your life. Quite often the picture comes up when you have other pictures indicating disappointment. The ANGEL gently reminds you to expand your vision, look beyond your problem. You may have problems in one aspect of your life, yet you are fortunate in having someone who will soothe your hurts.

The picture may also come up for a person who is acting in negative ways. You may be caught up in a situation where you are lying, cheating, drinking too much, or generally doing something negative. Yet the people close to you still love you and are willing to comfort you. Look around you and see who is offering the love and comfort that you need right now.

POSITION 4: Heavenly powers will save you from a false step. This refers to the universal goodness that exists. In times of trouble or indecision, it is difficult to know what the right step is. However, if you evaluate your situation honestly and act according to what you believe is right and honest, then you will take the correct path.

The heavenly powers are like the angel that sits on your shoulder and points the right way. The angel counteracts the negative urging of the devil, who sits on your other shoulder. The devil urges you to false or self-centered actions, while the angel leads you to good, altruistic actions. When you get the ANGEL picture in this position, you know that goodness prevails. You have tapped into the universal good, with the result that your actions will be correct.

38   LADY

PERIOD OF INFLUENCE: short

SYMBOL FOR: support, help

MEANING: ↓ 1. A soft feminine hand will support you in time.
            → 2. The helping hand is given to you not in friendship but due to hidden love.
            ← 3. Don't believe the show of politeness; it is false.
            ↑ 4. Having sucked you dry, they will turn away from you.

GENERAL MEANING OF PICTURE: The LADY in the cards symbolizes a feminine force that gives you help and insight. In Homer's Odyssey, the goddess Circe first tricked Odysseus, or Ulysses, but later gave him advice that helped him on his journey home. The LADY in the cards looks like she is a married woman but need not be; she is someone who is mature in outlook and wise enough to give you good advice or simply be there when you need her. Unlike the ANGEL picture, which symbolizes spiritual support, the LADY picture means down-to-earth, practical support. The lady could be your mother, mother-in-law, grandmother, friend, co-worker, or anyone who is close enough to help you. When males get this picture, the main idea of support is true for them also. However, in position 2, there is a hint of love present. In the last two positions, the picture expresses the negative aspects of the feminine mystique.

POSITION 1: A soft feminine hand will support you in time. This picture comes up quite often for people who are having difficulties. The helping hand usually belongs to someone close to you, but sometimes it can belong to someone you don't expect at all, even a stranger who is there when you need him or her. For example, you may be going through a difficult time in your life and be too embarrassed to talk to anyone close, when a social acquaintance may sense your hurt and give you the support you need. Or it may be that a family member whom you are not even close to will come to your aid during a family crisis. Somehow these people know that you need help and they are there, unquestioning and uncritical. When you get this picture, you know that you have support, so look around you, see who is there, and use that person's strength to get you through the difficult time.

POSITION 2: Someone is giving you a helping hand not out of friendship but due to hidden love. The picture can refer to either a man or a woman who is offering the help. Whether a man or a woman gets the picture, it means someone is helping you, giving you support, but for an ulterior reason—hidden love. If all you want is support, then accept it, because it is given genuinely. However, keep in mind that the other person likes you, so don't do anything unwise to hurt his or her feelings. Quite often when males and females work together or are good friends, sexual tension is present. This is normal and just means that we are vibrant individuals and the opposite sex appreciates us. We don't have to fall in love or have a love affair, as this will most likely ruin the friendship or working relationship. In the last decade, women have been criticized for using men's support to advance in the work force or in society, yet men have been supported by women just as much over the ages. In fact, both sexes have survived because of each other's support from time immemorial.

The picture can also refer to someone much younger having a puppy-love crush on you. You might not even be aware of this person's existence. When the picture comes up, look around you, see who it could refer to, but don't do anything that may hurt or embarrass the person unnecessarily. A well-known Russian proverb states: Don't spit into the well; you may need to drink the water. Today, when age barriers are crumbling, it's good to have friends of various ages.

POSITION 3: Don't believe the show of politeness; it is false. This could refer to a work, social, or personal situation. This is not necessarily a bad omen, as we are all taught to be polite at all times. Just remember if you get the picture in this position, to accept the politeness or kindness, but not to divulge any personal information at this time, as this person is not your real friend.

POSITION 4: Having sucked you dry, they will turn away from you. This can refer to work, social, or personal relationships. For example, children may drain you of money, exhaust you from all their demands, and then leave without so much as a thank you for all your efforts. Spouses or co-workers may do the same. However, rather than despairing, you should rejoice. This is a time to stop being a slave to others' demands and to begin a period of self-pampering and self-discovery. You have been giving too much of yourself to others. Perhaps they needed the help in the beginning, but now your help is unwanted and unappreciated. Therefore, congratulate yourself on having been a good support, as no one will, and go on with your life. We would all like to be thanked for our efforts, but people are careless or plain stupid and forget to express appreciation, with the result that we feel hurt or used. When this happens, accept it, acknowledge the hurt, and go on with your life. At least the burden of helping someone else is gone and you have free time to devote to your interests and desires.

39 HORSE

PERIOD OF INFLUENCE: immediate

SYMBOL FOR: emotional upheaval

MEANING: ↓ 1. You will experience a vivid or traumatic life event.
  → 2. Outward appearance and beauty will turn your head.
  ← 3. Hold the reins firmly; otherwise, you will stumble.
  ↑ 4. Your feelings will be trampled upon.

GENERAL MEANING OF PICTURE: The horse is a very powerful animal. From earliest times, humans have admired the intelligent, sensible, noble, proud horse. In Greek mythology, the first horse, the winged steed Pegasus, sprang from the union of the god Poseidon and Medusa. Pegasus, together with his rider, were instrumental in exterminating the Chimaera, a voracious fire-eating monster that symbolizes humankind's passions and basic earthly nature. At another time, Pegasus stamped his hoof to create the fountain of the Muses. Thus the horse has evolved as a powerful symbol of enlightenment and extermination of evil forces. At the same time, taming of the horse led to tremendous upheavals in the world. Once the horse was used for transportation, great migrations resulted. But even more significant was human use of the horse for military purposes. Civilizations like that of the Aztecs were destroyed by a relatively few Spaniards riding horses. Therefore, the horse can symbolize either intelligence and enlightenment or brutal destructive powers.

In the cards, the HORSE stands for our emotions. In the same way that the HORSE is powerful, so are our emotions. They drive us to success or despair, depending on how we learn to use them. The picture warns us of a powerful emotional experience that is to occur.

It may be a happy event or a sad one. It is up to us whether to react to it in a positive or negative way.

POSITION 1: You will experience a vivid or traumatic life event. This can be either a good or a bad experience. The picture has appeared for people when they were about to get married, have a baby, get a new job, or get divorced, fired, scared, or let down emotionally by someone. It is hard for the person doing the reading to know what the picture refers to, but usually the person whose fortune is being read has an idea.

The vivid experience could be meeting or hearing an inspiring person who can change your whole outlook on life. It could be coming across a religious message or an intellectual idea that you find inspiring. You will feel uplifted and happy. Even meeting a famous actor or singer can cause the same euphoric feeling.

The picture may also refer to outside events—events in the political, economic or even environmental spheres that we react to emotionally. For example, many people experienced John Kennedy's assassination as a traumatic event. One time the picture appeared for a friend of mine who was going home to California. A couple of days later, there was an earthquake where she lived. She had had no pictures warning her of danger, only this picture warning her of a traumatic experience. During the earthquake, although she was emotionally upset, she was rational enough to do all the correct things. No harm came to her or to anyone with her.

POSITION 2: Outward appearance and beauty will turn your head. This can most certainly refer to a romantic interest. You will meet someone whose beauty or handsomeness will appeal to you. You will throw caution aside. If there are no other pictures warning you of danger, then enjoy the situation for what it is. However, pay heed to the Russian proverb: Love is blind—you can even fall in love with a goat. Perhaps you should seek a second opinion from a friend before plunging headlong into a relationship with this new exquisite being.

The picture can also refer to other things that you are attracted to for their outward appearance, such as a race horse you want to bet on or a house you want to buy. The picture doesn't tell you that it is bad to be emotionally drawn to beautiful things; it just tells you to be aware that you are more emotional than rational at this stage.

POSITION 3: Hold the reins firmly; otherwise, you will stumble. A person in a wagon with twenty horses pulling it has to have a firm hand on the reins; otherwise, the horses may go in different directions, causing the driver and the wagon to tumble. In your daily life you seldom have to drive a team of horses, yet you do get involved with many activities and your emotions are pulled in twenty different directions. The picture tells you to hold on tightly; don't give in to the pressure or exert unnecessary energy in any one area. It is good to remember that this picture refers to your immediate situation, that the emotional turmoil will end, just like the team of horses has to come to a stop. The important thing is to keep the emotions intact, to channel them to a positive conclusion. When the picture appears, most people know what it is referring to. It is a reminder to them of the necessity to take control of the situation or to ease up.

Parents sometimes get overly involved with the activities of their children. They can run themselves and the children ragged trying to do everything. Perhaps it is time to ease up, cut down on the number of activities, so that you can enjoy what you are doing.

POSITION 4: Your feelings will be trampled upon. This is an external action over which you have little control. Your spouse, lover, child, or parent will do something that will hurt you. This person either will not care or will not realize that he or she has hurt you. Those closest to you usually hurt you the most, but the picture also can refer to other people in your life such as teachers, employers, or even friends. You can't do anything to avoid the hurt, only brace yourself to minimize the pain.

40 KNOT

PERIOD OF INFLUENCE: life

SYMBOL FOR: family ties

MEANING: ↓ 1. You have tied strong knots for a lifetime.
→ 2. The chains binding you will always be sweet.
← 3. You will break the bonds that are entangling you.
↑ 4. You can achieve freedom only by cutting the Gordian knot.

GENERAL MEANING OF PICTURE: A knot can join two pieces of rope, or it can create a lump or knob in a single piece of rope. The KNOT picture is a symbol for union, strong bonds that bind us, especially in marriage. It can also represent entanglements, problems that bind us and prevent us from doing what we would like to do. The bonds can be applied externally, by other people, or internally, by ourselves. Our attitude toward the bonds can determine whether they are positive or negative.

POSITION 1: You have tied strong knots for a lifetime. The picture usually refers to family bonds of a positive nature. You have a very positive relationship with your parents, spouse, children, siblings, or other family members. The picture could refer to a strong bond with a friend, but usually the DOG would indicate that. The picture appears at times when you may be having problems in a relationship. The picture tells you that regardless of the problems, you have formed a bond that will transcend them. The literal translation of the picture is: You have tied strong knots for centuries. For those who believe in reincarnation, this would imply that the bonds go beyond this life-

139

time, that you may have been in some kind of relationship with this person in previous lives. The problems may arise because you do have differences that need to be resolved sometimes.

The picture is always reassuring, as it indicates you are not alone. There are people who genuinely care for you, and with their help you are much stronger and can do more than if you were alone. The knot ties two separate parts into a longer and stronger entity.

POSITION 2: The chains or bonds binding you will always be sweet. The terms *chains* or *bonds* usually have negative connotations. Yet chains or bonds can also be positive. Children are like chains because once you have a child, he or she is a part of your life whether you like it or not till death. The same applies to other family relationships. In position 2, the picture tells you that these bonds will always be gentle or pleasant. If you have children, then for the most part you will get along with them and they will be a support to you in your lifetime. If the picture refers to your partner or spouse, then it means you have a good strong relationship that will nurture you.

The picture can refer to other obligations or duties in life that you have to perform. Perhaps you have chosen a career that demands your total dedication, such as the ministry, medicine, teaching, or the arts. The picture tells you that the duties will not seem onerous; rather, you will enjoy them. This could be the result of your own positive personality in that you always look on the bright side, or it could be that your job will be gratifying, full of unexpected pleasures.

POSITION 3: You will break the bonds that are entangling you. The picture is positive in that it tells you, you will be able to release yourself from bondage. The entanglement can be a relationship that you are involved in. The picture does not say that you will break up the relationship, only that you will break the bonds that are entangling you. For example, you have been preparing dinner for your family at six o'clock for the last twenty years. Now there is an exercise class at that time that you would like to join. The picture tells you that you will find a solution; you can take the exercise class and someone else will take over your obligation of preparing the dinner. The picture further indicates not only that the physical aspect of preparing the dinner will be done by someone else, but your mental feeling of obligation will be gone as well.

You are your own worst enemy at times. You impose more obligations on yourself, set more deadlines, and have higher expectations than other people have of you. Some of the expectations have been instilled by your parents, others by the expectations of society or even by advertising. For example, you might find yourself more concerned and obsessive about housecleaning than you should be. Or perhaps you are fixing your car for the hundredth time, when it should be junked. These are bonds that complicate your life rather than simplify it. Thus the picture tells you that whether the bond that is binding you is a person, a situation, or your own expectations, you will be able to break it.

POSITION 4: You can achieve freedom only by cutting the Gordian knot. The Gordian knot is told about in Greek mythology. A poor peasant named Gordius became king of Phrygia. He dedicated his wagon to the greatest god, Zeus. The pole of the wagon was fastened to the yoke for the animals by a very complicated knot. The oracle foretold that the man who could loosen this knot would be ruler of Asia. Many tried to untie the knot, but failed. Then Alexander the Great came to the city and very simply cut the knot with one blow of his sword; he then went on to conquer Asia. The lesson for us is that sometimes when we have a problem, we need to take a decisive action, make a clean break, to solve it.

This is not the time to talk about the situation, to think, rationalize, plead, or use any other stalling method. Make a clean break, and then walk away from the situation. In a relationship, the other person might use charm, pleas, or threats of suicide to keep you. When this picture comes up, it tells you not to give in, to stick to your principles and do what you have to do. You may hurt the other person, but you will hurt yourself more by giving in.

In business it is sometimes better to cut your losses than to keep on sinking funds into a losing proposition. By making a clean break at this time, you will find future success.

41 CAT

PERIOD OF INFLUENCE: short

SYMBOL FOR: hidden danger

MEANING: ↓ 1. Someone will charm you with kindness, which you'll yield to.
→ 2. Beware of claws hidden beneath a friendly exterior.
← 3. Having received a blow, you will hide your feelings with dignity.
↑ 4. You will unexpectedly be badly scratched.

GENERAL MEANING OF PICTURE: The cat was first domesticated in Egypt about twenty-six hundred years ago. The ancient Egyptians believed cats were sacred. They worshiped a goddess named Bastet, whom they pictured with the body of a woman and the head of a cat. However, cats have not always been well liked. During the Dark Ages in Europe, many people were afraid of cats. They thought cats had magical powers and were the friends of witches. Today cats live all over the world as household pets. Yet even though the cat has been domesticated for such a long time, it still maintains its wild characteristics and can strike out at any time. The CAT picture represents someone who can be charming to you, or can turn around and unexpectedly scratch you. "Catty" characteristics have been associated with female behavior; however, men can and do behave in the same fashion.

POSITION 1: Someone will charm you, and you will yield to it. When a cat wants something, it rubs your leg, purrs, and follows you until you satisfy its needs. Usually it is so charming that you gladly do it. The picture tells you that someone will be very charming to you in the same way. It could be your son or daughter who is being so nice to you because he or she wants an advance on allowance or some other favor. Or it could be your co-worker who is buttering you up for a favor.

The person who is being charming doesn't necessarily need a favor immediately. Cats can be charming and purr at various times, as long as they are well fed and taken care of. The picture in this position doesn't warn you of any danger; therefore, enjoy the praise and charm, but be aware that the person laying it on could have an alternative purpose. All of us behave in this way to some extent, being nice to people who someday may be of help to us.

POSITION 2: Beware of claws hidden beneath a friendly exterior. The cat sleeping can be a picture of serenity, but if you touch it, it can claw you. People also can be provoked to mean actions. The picture warns you that someone around you who is very charming and friendly also can be dangerous. In the work place this can be one of your co-workers or your immediate supervisor. This person can be very friendly, but if you infringe on his or her territory, he or she will strike back immediately, either with verbal barbs or some action that blocks your career advancement. When the picture comes up in this position, be very careful that you don't ruffle other people's feathers as you will be the one who will be hurt.

The picture also can refer to people you run into who seem very friendly but can turn on you for no apparent reason. Psychopaths are charming and then turn around and do all kinds of evil actions without remorse. The person with claws can be someone you know or a new acquaintance. When the picture comes up in this position, be very careful who you are with and don't be too trusting of friendly strangers.

POSITION 3: Having received a blow, you will hide your feelings with dignity. The blow can be bad news of any kind. Perhaps you have been fired, found out your spouse is cheating on you, failed a test, found out you have some illness, or simply been slighted. Regardless of the bad news, you will be able to hide your feelings with dignity. By doing so, you are giving yourself time to adjust to the situation without outside interference. Everyone likes a winner and avoids losers. By acting like a winner, even in adversity, you gain the respect of others and improve your chances of recouping the loss. Remember: You are greeted according to your clothes, but accompanied according to your mind. Therefore, behave in your most dignified way at this time.

POSITION 4: You will unexpectedly be badly scratched. This usually refers to a verbal attack or a catty remark that someone makes to you. It is usually unprovoked by you and not deserved. The best way to act is not to get angry or upset, but simply to ask the person, "Why are you saying this?" This puts the onus of justifying the remark on the person. Silence is also a good rebuttal to catty remarks. Don't give the person the pleasure of seeing you get irritated or disturbed.

You should also be wise enough to avoid provoking a verbal attack. Refrain from boorish acts that irritate people, like dropping in uninvited. The Russians say: An uninvited guest is worse than a Tartar. The Tartars were Mongolian invaders of Russia during the Middle Ages. If you behave boorishly, expect to be criticized.

42 SCALES

PERIOD OF INFLUENCE: short to life

SYMBOL FOR: justice, balance

MEANING: ↓ 1. In your fate, good will outweigh evil.
→ 2. Your happiness depends on the decision you make.
← 3. If you maintain your balance, you will come out whole from a predicament.
↑ 4. Your evil action will have consequences.

GENERAL MEANING OF PICTURE: The scales of balance have been used for thousands of years to weigh goods. When the scales are used properly, then fairness prevails. Conversely, when the scales are used in an unfair way, then injustice occurs. Thus over the years, the scales have become the symbol for justice. The law courts use the symbol of a woman holding the scales to represent justice. This picture likewise reminds you of justice and stirs your actions toward the good.

POSITION 1: In your life or fate, good will outweigh evil. This is a life picture and a very positive one. For those who believe in reincarnation, this card tells you that you have good karma. You will do more good in life and consequently more good will come your way than evil. This doesn't mean that you will never do evil or have it done to you, but that the good is a much stronger force and will in the end outweigh any evil that comes your way. This picture can be very reassuring to people who are caught up in an unfair situation. It is good to know that in the end, as long as you stay true to your beliefs and as long as your own actions are good, you will be vindicated.

POSITION 2: If you make the correct decision, you will be happy. It is always difficult to know if the decisions you make are correct or not, yet if you keep in mind that this picture stands for justice, then your decisions will be easier to make. In today's society, where moral values are being attacked all the time, our leaders show weaknesses, and we see greed and injustice rewarded, it becomes somewhat difficult to know what is good and evil. Yet, there is an intrinsic part of you that knows the difference and can guide you in all circumstances. If you have lost touch with your own nature, then you can look to the Ten Commandments in the Bible, the moral teachings of other religions and cultures, or the laws of our country. They represent the common good toward which we should strive. Thus the picture tells you that in making your decision, you should strive toward the good. As an example, if you are given more money than is due you at the bank, should you keep it or give it back? You can rationalize that the bank makes lots of money and won't miss the small amount, yet is this correct? What about the teller who made the mistake—will she suffer consequences? And what about yourself? You will enjoy the money, but how long will you feel guilty? What is the good action in this case? Will you get greater happiness by keeping the money or by having a clear conscience? Ultimately it is up to you to make the choice, but you must remember that not all rich people are happy.

On the other hand, the picture does not tell you to surrender your own principles or to sell yourself short in favor of other people. Quite the opposite; you are the best judge of what is good for you. As long as your actions are just, you will make the correct decision, which will lead to happiness.

POSITION 3: The picture warns you to maintain your balance in order to get out of a difficult situation. This is not a time to vent your frustrations by having a tantrum. Instead, use your common sense, examine the situation carefully, and do what is right without too much recrimination or protestation. An example of what can happen when we don't maintain our balance is what happened to a friend of mine. His wife got into a very difficult financial circumstance. My friend had to resolve the situation, which he did well, but at the same time he unleashed all his frustrations in verbal attacks on his wife. Although the financial situation resolved itself, the marriage broke up due to the emotional havoc brought about by the uncontrolled verbal abuse. Had my friend been able to control his feelings, he would be much happier today.

146

The picture is positive in that it tells you that you will be able to overcome your problems. Perhaps you have too many irons in the fire and should eliminate everything but the essentials at this time. Even if you are doing a lot of good for society or your family, you sometimes get into situations that demand too much of your energy and can be a detriment to your health. Remember, by keeping your balance, you will come out whole from the predicament.

POSITION 4: Your evil action will have consequences. This could be a serious offense that you are committing, or a minor action that you are not even aware is evil. I've never done a reading for anyone who has committed a serious crime, but I presume that for those people, the repercussion would be imprisonment or an unhappy life. However, the picture also refers to the little acts of evil that you are tempted to do consciously or unconsciously. You might be tempted to tell people off for the hurt they caused you, or not invite them to a party, stand them up, not prepare dinner or do the wash for them, or take some other petty action that you know will hurt them. Sometimes you unintentionally hurt other people by imposing your standards of behavior on them. The Russian proverb says: Don't sit in other people's sleds. Don't tell others how they should behave.

When this picture comes up for you, be aware that your evil actions at this time will bring more harm to you than to the other person. Perhaps it is better at this time to turn the other cheek. For example, be careful while driving; don't cut people off or make obscene gestures to other drivers when they have done something to annoy you. Recently people have been shot for doing so. Getting wounded or killed is too high a price to pay for the small injustice you feel was done to you.

43 CRAYFISH

PERIOD OF INFLUENCE: short to life

SYMBOL FOR: learning to cope with fate

MEANING: ↓ 1. Having made too bold a step, you'll back off.
→ 2. Your pride will be hurt.
← 3. Delay is sometimes designed by fate.
↑ 4. Too much haste often defeats the business.

GENERAL MEANING OF PICTURE: The crayfish is a small crustacean that lives under rocks in rivers and ponds. It is a scavenger, eating anything found in the waters. At the same time, it is prey to larger fish and especially humans, who find it delicious. The CRAY-FISH picture represents fate: being in the right place and doing the right thing. As the crayfish is sandwiched between being a predator and a victim, so we find ourselves caught up in situations where we want to do one thing but fate doesn't open up the opportunity. The picture may have a short period of influence, but in position 3, it explains happenings that affect your entire life. The SCYTHE also relates to fate, but it warns you of external forces over which you have little control. The CRAYFISH deals more with your emotional reactions to what fate deals out to you. It shows ways of dealing with setbacks that you will encounter in life.

POSITION 1: Having made too bold a step, you'll back off. The picture usually comes up in this position when you have more than one way of dealing with a situation. For example, you need to travel to a destination. Should you drive or take the plane? You want to take the car because it will give you more freedom, but if you take the

148

plane you will be more rested and will lose fewer working days. Your emotions take over and you decide to drive. You make all the arrangements, but at the last moment reason takes over and you back down. When the picture comes up in this position, it usually indicates that you are not really ready to make the move, or that fate doesn't want you to make this move at this time. The picture can refer to major moves such as emigrating to a new country, or minor ones like deciding not to go on a date with a new friend. Whatever the step is that you have to back off from, you should not feel guilty as this is simply not the right time for your action.

POSITION 2: Your pride will be hurt. In the same way as crayfish are prey to larger fish, so you are vulnerable to other people's opinions, especially if these people are higher up than you are. Whatever you take pride in—your job, family, house, business, sport, or self— will be criticized by someone. The criticism will seem unfair and hurt you, yet there will be some truth in what the person is saying. The Russian proverb warns: If you call yourself a mushroom, climb into the basket. If you say you are an important person, then prove it with your action. Perhaps you have been guilty of exaggeration or not doing what you said you would do. You should be open enough to listen attentively to the censure, so that you can work on correcting whatever you've been doing wrong that you were perhaps not even aware of. You see yourself one way; others may not see the same image. If they tell you that you are projecting a negative image, then you should work on improving it.

POSITION 3: Delay is sometimes designed by fate. This picture appears in this position when you want something, but it doesn't materialize. For example, you might want to have a child, a promotion at work, a new car, or something else that you think will add to your life's happiness. The picture tells you that this is not the right time for you to get what you want. Don't waste your energies fighting the situation, as the delay is meant by fate and you are powerless to change it. If you push too hard, you can create a worse situation. If you let go, you will get what you want when the time is right, and it can be even better than you first envisioned.

The picture also refers to intangible states of mind produced by a delay. That is, perhaps coping with a delay will lead you to discover the meaning of love, patience, faithfulness, kindness, or mercy in

149

your life. Perhaps this is the lesson that you have to learn in this lifetime. This is a very personal message and only the person who receives the picture will know what it refers to. What is it in your life right now that is presenting itself as a problem, and what are you learning from the experience?

POSITION 4: Too much haste often defeats the business. The meaning is the same as the proverb "Haste makes waste." The picture tells you to slow down, to be more careful in what you are doing. By giving yourself time, you will do a much better job. The picture can refer to any project or idea that you have, whether painting your house, sewing a dress, fixing your car, starting a business, writing a book, making a proposal at work, or rushing into a relationship. The MOON picture in position 4 tells you that delay will work against you, while the CRAYFISH picture in this position tells you that careful, diligent action on your part is needed at this time. In fact, the activity may be delayed even for years without any loss in the final outcome. Remember, just as the crayfish may get eaten if it leaves its protective rocks, so our ideas and projects if presented prematurely may be taken over by others or rejected. Therefore, perfect what you have first, and only then venture forth.

44   FIRE

PERIOD OF INFLUENCE: short to middle

SYMBOL FOR: passion

MEANING: ↓ 1. Fire will envelop your heart.
→ 2. Beware of fire, you'll burn your wings.
← 3. Out of the frying pan into the fire.
↑ 4. You will be warmed by love during difficult, cold days.

GENERAL MEANING OF PICTURE: Our first reaction to fire is that it is a destructive force. Once a fire takes hold, it is difficult to stop or contain until it burns itself out. So it is with people's passion. Once passion is ignited, it is difficult to stop. Even though unexpected fire can cause a lot of damage, fire was one of humankind's first and greatest discoveries. The ability to control fire and use it in constructive ways enabled humans to leave the Stone Age. So it is with passion. Passion has inspired some of the best works of art, literature, music, architecture, and engineering. Fire can also indicate flourishment—the flourishment of ideas or business ventures. It can also indicate the passion of our hearts. The picture warns that passion will take hold of you; it is up to you to use it for positive results.

POSITION 1: Fire will envelop your heart. This fire or passion can refer to a romantic interest, or it can refer to any other consuming interest or pursuit. If it is a romantic interest, then you will most likely meet a person who will wildly excite you, will stir up your passions or sexually arouse you. If you are already involved in a situation or are married, the picture implies you could meet someone new, or it could be that your relationship with your partner will reach a new high where passions are unleashed. The picture's influence is of rather short duration, as passion cannot endure for a long time without burning itself out, so enjoy it to the utmost.

In position 1 there is no warning of danger, so that the passion is good for your soul. If the picture does not refer to a romantic interest, then it points to something in your life at this time that you are totally involved in. It could be your work, your sport, or anything else that stirs your passion. The picture tells you to let the passion reign, take advantage of the beneficial uses of fire. It is interesting that in Chinese philosophy, fire is a good sign; it indicates flourishment much like the sun provides. Also, bad spirits are kept away by the fire. Thus if the FIRE comes up for you in position 1, take advantage of it while you have the chance.

POSITION 2: Beware of fire, you will burn your wings. Here the picture refers to the Greek myth of Icarus. His father made them wings of feathers and wax to escape imprisonment. Against the advice of his father, Icarus flew too close to the sun. The heat melted his wings and he plunged into the sea and drowned. Icarus let pride, vanity, and ambition surpass his judgment and his father's advice. The picture warns you of the destructive nature of both fire and your own passions if left unchecked.

The picture may be telling you that your ambitions are unrealistic at this time. Perhaps you have an inflated view of yourself. These unrealistic expectations will bring harm only to yourself. Don't operate beyond your capabilities. If you are seeking a job, it may be a good idea at this time to settle for something less than what you want. Otherwise you may end up with no job at all.

The picture also tells you to control your passions. If you get involved with someone you shouldn't be involved with, such as in an adulterous liaison, you will burn your wings. Your marriage will suffer or public scandal will result. If you let your passions in other areas get out of control, you will likewise suffer. Vincent van Gogh, one of the great artists, painted with passionate zeal; yet his uncontrolled passion led to his cutting off his own ear, and later to his mental illness and untimely death. Thus when this picture comes up in position 2, you should be very careful of the passion that possesses you, as it can bring you more harm than good.

POSITION 3: You will go from the frying pan into the fire. You are in a hot position right now, and it will only intensify in heat. The only way to rescue a piece of meat that slips from the frying pan into the fire is to quickly remove it from the fire. If you hesitate and leave it in, it will burn and be useless. Thus it is with you; whatever you are involved in is getting out of hand and should be abandoned at this time. If it is a love relationship, then it is leading to destruction and should be stopped. If it is a business venture, then it is a time to pull back and consolidate your gains rather than expand. You can always go back to the project later, as you can put the meat back in the frying pan if it is not cooked enough. At the present moment, realize that quick decisions and actions are necessary on your part to save the day. Some people enjoy intense heat and can flourish in it, but to most of us the picture is a warning of danger.

POSITION 4: You will be warmed by love during difficult, cold days. This is the positive aspect of fire. In the same way that fire gives you warmth in the winter, so love can keep you warm during difficult times. This picture came up for a family that was moving to a Third World country for a number of years. It seemed strange, as they were going to a tropical country and everyone was looking forward to the adventure. However, during their stay they witnessed many troubling things; it was a difficult period of time for them. Yet when they came back, the family was so unified that it was a pleasure to witness. Love kept them together during their individual difficult experiences.

The picture is unsettling in that it warns you of difficult times to come, yet it is reassuring in that it says love will keep you warm during those times. There are always wars, depressions, recessions, and troubles that people are forced to endure, but love can make them tolerable and even memorable experiences. Many enjoyable evenings have been spent hearing stories from parents and grandparents about war, where love and ingenuity have overcome difficulty.

45 PIG

PERIOD OF INFLUENCE: immediate to middle

SYMBOL FOR: earthly pleasures

MEANING: ↓ 1. Positively a prosperous and happy year.
→ 2. Purely an earthly happiness.
← 3. Your greed will be punished.
↑ 4. Overindulgence in food will make you sick.

GENERAL MEANING OF PICTURE: The pig is a symbol of prosperity. In the past, it was the rich farmer who had pigs. Owning pigs guaranteed a steady supply of food. On the negative side, the pig symbolizes greed and avarice.

The picture suggests material wealth, plenty to eat, contentment, and earthly pleasures; a life free of strife and worry.

POSITION 1: Positively a prosperous and happy year. The picture in this position is always welcome as it indicates a good year for you. It does not necessarily mean that you will get rich suddenly; rather, it means that within your present circumstances, you will be very comfortable. You will not have money problems. Life will be easy, comfortable, and free of any major economic problems.

POSITION 2: Purely an earthly happiness. The picture tells you to enjoy your earthly pleasures. This can be your house, parties, family gatherings, relationships, or material possessions. If you have purchased a new car or anything else, then enjoy it for the pleasure it gives you. The picture can also refer to the pleasures of a sexual relationship. Too often we let guilt feelings interfere with the sensations of pleasure. The picture tells you to enjoy what you have for the moment.

POSITION 3: Your greed will be punished. This is the negative aspect of the picture. It tells you to take only what you need at this time and let the rest be shared. It can also be warning that you want too many material possessions, a larger house than you need, a bigger car, or such. If you are going into debt for these possessions, then you should stop spending, lock up your charge cards, and wait until a more suitable time. Taking financial risks or speculating at this time is discouraged.

In a family situation, if you are demanding more money from your spouse or relatives than is necessary, it will result in bad feelings and arguments.

At work, if you are picking the choicest assignments, you will arouse antagonism from your co-workers. Be fair at this time; otherwise, you are doing harm to yourself in the long run.

Sexually, if you have more lovers than you need, you will get into trouble.

POSITION 4: Overindulgence in food will make you sick. If you have diabetes, ulcers, heart trouble, cancer, arthritis, gallstones, or any other ailment that is affected by diet, you should be very careful with your food intake when this picture appears.

In the past, I have had several gallstone attacks. I have kept the attacks under control by not eating fatty foods. This picture is always a warning to me that I am getting careless and that unless I go back to my diet, I will get sick.

Even if you do not suffer from any ailment, you should be more careful with your food and drink intake. Perhaps you are eating too much junk food and should start eating more healthy foods. Poor eating habits lead to many kinds of illnesses. The picture is telling you that your eating habits need improvement.

46 BRIDGE

PERIOD OF INFLUENCE: short to life

SYMBOL FOR: deliberate change

MEANING: ↓ 1. A radical change in lifestyle awaits you.
→ 2. You will build a bridge that will draw you together with a loved person.
← 3. No matter where you go the past will pursue you.
↑ 4. If you want freedom, create a bridge over the chasm.

GENERAL MEANING OF PICTURE: This is one of the life pictures. The bridge symbolizes our ability to change our circumstances. We often refer to life as a road. A bridge is an example of our manipulation of our environment, the ability to change the road we are on. We don't have to sit and wait for nature to take its course. Instead, we can change the environment to suit our purpose. This picture emphasizes that we have some control over our lives, that our will power is stronger than fate.

POSITION 1: A radical change in lifestyle awaits you. The picture appears when you have finished one phase of your life and are embarking on a new one. You have finished school and are beginning to work. Or maybe you are getting married, having a baby, or getting a promotion at work. In any case, your previous life is finished. Some people do not react favorably to change and may resent the new obligations and responsibilities; yet new joys and rewards are also in store.

This picture usually appears for me in June, at the end of a busy school year. It signifies that the long days of teaching and marking will soon be replaced by two months of idleness.

156

POSITION 2: You will build a bridge that will draw you together with a loved person. Your actions or will power can change your circumstances. In life sometimes we drift apart from our parents, lovers, children, or even close friends. The picture reminds you that at this particular time it is up to you to make the first move to ensure that the relationship endures. Make the move, build the bridge, and enjoy the rewards of a loving relationship.

A solid bridge that lasts takes a long time to construct. It is the same with good relationships. Spending time with your loved ones, celebrating holidays together, attending recitals or sports events together, are the building blocks that create strong relationships.

POSITION 3: No matter where you go the past will pursue you. You will not escape your problems by running away. It is better to face up to the situation and try to solve it than to run away.

The picture may refer to parents or children that you can't get rid of. They may have inflicted pain on you, and you are trying to avoid them. Yet, no matter what you do, they will stay in the picture. The best thing to do is to reconcile with them, so that they are not a negative influence in your life.

On the positive side, the picture may refer to good things that have happened to you in the past. Perhaps you were a national swimming champion, a good bridge player, an actor or actress, or excelled in some other field. The fame and glory of your early years will stay with you. You can ignore it or you can use it to your advantage.

The picture may also refer to a person you have known—a spouse, friend, or relative. The person may have died or gone away, yet the memory of him or her will stay with you always. It's good to have the memories, as long as they don't interfere with your present life.

POSITION 4: If you want freedom, create a bridge over the chasm. Seek a new solution to your problem. Rather than getting stuck in your problem, create a new bridge that will let you step over it. For example, if you are having marital problems, and communication or tears are not resolving the problem, try a new approach. Think back to find an activity the two of you truly enjoy together. If it is sex, then meet him or her at the door with a martini and nothing else; if it is dinner out, then make a reservation at the best gourmet restaurant; if it is going to ball games, buy two tickets and surprise him or her.

Doing things together that please both of you can bridge the gap no matter how wide it is.

Too often we get so bogged down in our problems that we forget there are solutions. If you can't think of anything yourself, then seek the advice of those who can help you. Counselors, psychiatrists, doctors, ministers are all trained and willing to help you understand and overcome your problems.

47 DEMONS

PERIOD OF INFLUENCE: short

SYMBOL FOR: subconscious negative thoughts

MEANING: ↓ 1. Do not listen to cunning whisperings wishing to hurt you.
→ 2. Yielding to the temptation of taking vengeance for an offense, you will only increase the unpleasantness.
← 3. Too much unrestrained merriment occurs before chagrin.
↑ 4. Your fervor will not lead to any good.

GENERAL MEANING OF PICTURE: Demons are your inner conflicts, the negative thoughts that cause doubt or urge retaliation. Sometimes the demons are the base side of your nature, which wants to strike back in a cruel or careless manner when you are hurt. As a child, I remember being told that the angel sits on one shoulder and protects your actions, while the devil sits on your other shoulder urging you to do evil deeds. We are all familiar with the saying "The devil made me do it."

The picture in all positions urges you to control the negative side of your nature, as it will only lead to further unpleasantness.

POSITION 1: Do not listen to cunning whisperings wishing to hurt you. Do not fall prey to negative thoughts, whether they are feelings of greed, jealousy, doubt, inadequacy, insecurity, or paranoia. These thoughts undermine your self-confidence. They are only within you and are not a reflection of the reality around you. In other words, you can be your own worst enemy. If the feelings are not checked, they

159

can torment you needlessly. Recently I visited a friend who enumerated all the bad points in his life. If he could have heard himself speaking, he would have realized what a negative image he was presenting to the world. No wonder bad things were happening to him.

One has to learn to listen to the negative thoughts, examine their warning, but then put the thoughts to rest and proceed with the positive action. There are good books on the market that can help with channeling positive energy.

Should you feel that you cannot control your negative thoughts, then you should seek professional help.

POSITION 2: Yielding to the temptation of taking vengeance for an offense, you will only increase the unpleasantness. This advice is like the Christian doctrine that tells you to turn the other cheek to an offense. The picture may refer to a situation at home, work, or in a relationship that you have.

You may find yourself on one side or another of a controversial issue such as abortion, or a particular strike. Each side thinks it is right, and the members may take actions that are offensive to the other side. In a strike situation, the work force may be divided in half. Those who support the company may be called all kinds of names, and vice versa. Should you be caught up in such a situation, don't yield to the temptation to take vengeance. Remember the strike will be over and you will have to work with the people on the other side.

Sometimes you will get this picture after you have already struck back at someone. In that case, cool down and act as politely and cordially as possible. The unpleasantness will clear up.

POSITION 3: Too much unrestrained merriment occurs before grief or chagrin. Don't do foolish things in the name of fun. Sometimes we drink too much, talk too much, or do something unlawful in the name of fun, but the next day we regret our actions. The picture doesn't tell you not to have a good time, only to be careful of your actions. If you are drinking, then don't drive, as accidents may occur.

Aging Lotharios thinking of spicing up their life with some new romance should pay heed to the Russian proverb: Gray hair in the beard, but the devil in the ribs. Adam got Eve from his rib. Some men, as they get older, begin to chase women. The picture warns you that what you think is fun—chasing women—may make you appear foolish in other people's eyes. Also, in today's society, indiscriminate and unprotected sex can lead to all kinds of infections and subsequent grief. The picture can apply to women's actions as well as men's.

POSITION 4: Your fervor, eagerness, enthusiasm, or hysterics will not bring you any good. If you are faced with a problem, deal with it in a rational way. Don't fall prey to irrational, frenzied activity that leads nowhere. The MOON picture in position 4 tells you that action is necessary, while this picture tells you that eagerness at this time defeats the purpose.

It has taken me many years to learn that my fervor in getting the house cleaned or fixed up by family members often results in arguments and the work not being done. If you want something done, do it yourself. But again, do not rush into any project, as in your eagerness you may not do the job properly and may have to redo it later.

When you get this picture, be especially aware of the negative statements you are making. You may have a right to be angry, but you should nevertheless restrain your verbal lashings. Problems get resolved, yet bitter words once released are hard to forget or forgive. In the same way, be careful of what you write down. The Russian proverb cautions: What is written by a quill can't be cut down by an ax. If you write a letter of resignation during an angry moment, it may be hard to undo once you have regained your senses. Remember, it's the devil, not the angel, that is urging your actions at this moment.

48 ROOSTER

PERIOD OF INFLUENCE: immediate

SYMBOL FOR: news that wakes you

MEANING: ↓ 1. Soon you will hear good news.
→ 2. Heart-to-heart sharing of news.
← 3. A cheerful pastime will force you to forget grief.
↑ 4. You will wake up from a sweet sleep to daily activity.

GENERAL MEANING OF PICTURE: The rooster crows at the beginning of day, signaling the coming of light. Once when a town was being secretly attacked at dawn, the rooster woke the residents in time to defend themselves. Thus the ROOSTER picture signals good news or a warning to defend yourself. It is a positive card, heralding significant news in regard to your daily life.

POSITION 1: Soon you will hear good news. It will be news that affects your home or daily life. It could be your child telling you she or he got an A on a spelling test, your neighbor having a party, getting positive results on your test, or any news that enlightens your day.

POSITION 2: Heart-to-heart sharing of news. You will be in a situation with either one other person or a group, where you will have a conversation about important feelings or occurrences in your life. The information you exchange will be important to both your lives. You may clarify your feelings toward each other or resolve a problem. The conversation will leave you with a good feeling, satisfied and happy. The talk can be with a relative, spouse, friend, or co-worker.

Quite often when good friends meet after being apart for a while, they have this kind of conversation, filling in the gaps of the missing years. The picture may refer to the reading that you are doing at the present time. The cards stimulate conversation and an exchange of common experiences, goals, and feelings among friends.

POSITION 3: A lively activity or cheerful pastime will force you to forget grief. Some grief, sorrow, or misfortune has affected your life. It may be a death, the absence of a loved person, children moving away, or such. You are powerless to change these natural rites of passage; however, you need not dwell on the grief. Pleasant activity will help you get over the grief. You can go to the movies, talk to friends, have a party, go camping, play bridge, exercise, or do anything else that makes you happy. By doing activities that you like, you will ease the sorrow that you cannot change.

POSITION 4: You will wake up from a sweet sleep to everyday matters. This is not a bad picture; rather, it reminds you of daily tasks you have been too busy to perform. Perhaps you have been spending too much time on one activity such as studying, exercising, or daydreaming. In the process you have ignored other daily activities such as taking out the garbage, cleaning the house, or fixing your car. The picture calls you to action. It is time to wake up and do the chores that have accumulated. Usually these things will be accomplished swiftly and successfully at this time.

49 DAGGER

PERIOD OF INFLUENCE: immediate

SYMBOL FOR: hidden assault

MEANING: ↓ 1. You will be protected in time.
→ 2. You will escape danger due to the concern of a friend.
← 3. You will experience a prick to your pride.
↑ 4. Someone will inflict pain on your heart.

GENERAL MEANING OF PICTURE: A dagger is a short, sharp weapon worn by knights and courtiers of old. Some hid it, while others wore it on their belts. The dagger symbolizes pain that can be inflicted on you by someone at any moment. The danger may be of a physical nature, or it may be a wound to your pride, self-esteem, vanity, or heart.

In the first two positions, the picture is actually a positive one, telling you that you will be protected in time.

POSITION 1: You will be protected in time. Someone is trying to hurt you, but because you will be protected in time, you might not even know of the threat. Police, firefighters, administrators, and government inspectors are always working, providing protection to society against many hidden dangers that we are unaware of. It could be criminals, or contaminated food, or dangerous facilities. Our taxes pay for protection, and you are benefiting from this. When you get this picture, make sure you listen to radio and television news and read the newspaper, so that you are aware of warnings given to the public. Pay attention to these warnings, as they are meant to protect you.

164

The picture may also refer to people wishing to hurt your reputation. Someone may be saying things behind your back, but another is standing up for you, defending your honor and actions. You may be totally unaware of the conversations. If the picture appears for you, make sure that all your actions are circumspect, and little harm will come your way.

POSITION 2: You will escape danger due to the concern of a friend. Again, because you will escape danger, you may not even be aware that there is any danger. The picture is reassuring. Recently I went on a long auto trip with a friend. I usually do a reading before going on trips. The picture came up in this position before the trip. We were to drive my friend's car, and I felt safe knowing that the car had been looked after. During the trip, my friend also gave me advice on how to pass trucks on the road. I was hesitant to take his advice, yet once I followed it, I realized it was much safer than what I had been doing. My entire trip was made more pleasurable because I didn't have to worry needlessly. I knew we would escape danger. Still, I was careful not to do anything foolish at this time.

POSITION 3: You will experience a prick to your pride. Your self-esteem or vanity will be hurt. You may be asked to do something that you excel at, yet when you do it, no one pays any attention to it or you. Or someone may criticize you at home, work, or in the community. The CAT picture in position 4 also refers to unexpected attacks. The DAGGER picture warns of a sharper and deeper attack, one that strikes at the basis of your being, deflates your ego, and makes you doubt your achievements. The best defense is to accept the criticism and bear it with dignity. Perhaps you need this reminder not to get overconfident. At least be thankful that you understood the barb. If you were too dense to understand, the Russians would say you can't sew the brain to the skin. That is, you can try to teach people, but if they don't understand, you can't do anything. The stupid will stay stupid. At this time, your pride may be hurt, but at least you can learn from the experience.

The picture also may refer to not being invited to some function or included in some activity. The slight hurts. However, there can be many reasons why you were left out, such as lack of space or forgetfulness on someone's part. Don't dwell on the matter. · The sooner you can forget it, the better off you will be.

POSITION 4: Someone will inflict pain on your heart. This may be your husband or wife, irresponsible children, or inconsiderate lovers. The other person may stay out all night, forget to phone you, lie, be unfaithful, or do other things that hurt you. You can do little to change the behavior of the other person; however, you can minimize your hurt by not letting it become the dominant force in your life. Accept the pain—it is part of being a loving and giving person—but rather than dwelling on it, pick something else to concentrate on. If you are a student, then start declining French verbs or the parts of the human muscular structure. Paint your house, polish the car, find the most difficult pattern and sew a new outfit, do anything that will absorb your energy and thought. The pain will go away eventually and you will have a new skill or accomplishment as well.

Sometimes relationships last in spite of the pain that is inflicted at certain times. The pain may lead you to change your value system and bring a greater understanding to your relationship.

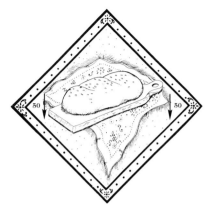

50 BREAD

PERIOD OF INFLUENCE: middle

SYMBOL FOR: happiness

MEANING: ↓ 1. You will be made happy with a present.
→ 2. Profit and happiness in the house, success in business affairs.
← 3. Fulfillment of wishes.
↑ 4. Having received something yourself, do not forget those surrounding you.

GENERAL MEANING OF PICTURE: Bread is the staff of life. The cultivation of grain has led to the formation of a stable society; thus, bread implies stability, prosperity, generosity, and nourishment. Christ was able to feed a multitude of people with a few loaves of bread. When you receive this picture, it means that your life and home are lucky; you are prosperous and content.

POSITION 1: You will be made happy with a present. The picture quite often comes up just before birthdays or other celebrations that we observe by giving presents. The picture implies that you will receive some present that you will enjoy. The present doesn't necessarily have to be an expensive one; rather, it is something that you truly like. The present may also be a total surprise, making you unexpectedly happy. As you are doing the reading, you already might have received the present, as the picture refers to events that may have happened in the past week or are to come very shortly.

Accept the present graciously even though you might worry about whether the person could really afford it. The present is given from the heart, and you make the giver happy by accepting it. Follow the Russian proverb: When you are given, take it; when you are beaten, run.

POSITION 2: Profit and happiness in the house, success in business affairs. This is a wonderful picture to get, especially if you are doing a reading for the year to come. The picture tells you that everything is going great for you. Financially you are well off. You might not be as rich as the people we see on TV, but you are happy with what you have. You have enough to give you a contented sense of well-being. The picture also implies that everyone else in your home is favored as well, thus creating a cheerful, harmonious household.

The picture tells you also that you have success in business. If you have a business, then it is doing very well. Profits are coming in. It is a good time to expand or try new ventures, as they will meet with success. For those who are working for someone else, it is also a favored time. This is a good time to seek promotions, suggest new ideas, or generally be in the public eye. Whatever business venture you begin now will meet with success.

POSITION 3: Fulfillment of wishes. The picture in this position is similar to the HORSESHOE and CLOVER pictures, which also promise that your wishes will come true. Some people have a hard time believing or accepting that good fortune is theirs for the taking. There are many good books on the market now teaching people how to visualize or make maps to achieve what they desire. Nothing is impossible. Christ was able to feed the masses with only a few loaves of bread. Make wishes, believe in them, and they will be fulfilled. Your wish could be as simple as having your kitchen painted or as difficult as saving the blue whale from becoming extinct. Generally, the BREAD picture refers to wishes that have a direct bearing on the quality of your life as well as that of humanity.

POSITION 4: Having received something yourself, do not forget those surrounding you. The picture is a gentle reminder to share your fortune with others. Having received a raise, don't forget to give some to charitable organizations. Having received a present, send a thank-you card so that the giver is also made happy. If receiving letters or phone calls from your friends makes you happy, then give back some of the joy by writing or phoning them yourself. In our busy everyday life we quite often forget the niceties of old, reciprocating for what we have received. Yet, a debt paid is happiness. Besides, what a wonderful circle we can create: someone does something nice for us, we in turn make them happy by responding, and they are more likely to do something nice again. The circle can continue indefinitely, bringing happiness and good will to everyone concerned. Generosity, even on the smallest scale, has far-reaching results. The Russians say: If everyone gives a thread, the naked one will have a shirt. Do your share of giving in some way.

PART III

EXAMPLES
OF
READINGS

ABOUT THE EXAMPLES

The examples included in this part were done for various individuals over many years. Only the names have been left out to protect the privacy of the individuals. I've included the examples for two purposes: first, to show how to write up a reading, and second, to show how to interpret the total card reading.

When you do a reading it is a good idea to write down the results. Put the date on the page for future reference and then list the pictures that appear, their positions, and their meanings, as shown in the examples. The reason for writing the reading down is to make you spend some time concentrating on yourself. All too often we run around doing errands and chores for everyone but ourselves. When we do spend time on ourselves, it's often in self-criticism. The cards always show the best in you. They indicate your strengths and call you to positive action.

When going over the examples, you will see that even in the most difficult times, positive pictures appear. The cards are your psychic barometer. They indicate the good and bad vibrations around you. When you are in a difficult time in your life, they will show that. However, they will also indicate possible solutions or support that you may be unaware of. Conversely, during a good period they may show problem areas you are not conscious of. By writing the message down, you are consciously becoming aware of the negative and positive things in your life. At the same time, your unconscious or higher inner self comes forth giving you new insights into the situation. As mentioned in the introduction, the pictures are metaphors for your life. Seeing your problems or achievements in the cards makes it easier to accept them.

It is always fun to look back at past readings. You can do as I have done in the examples and write a summary for each reading. You will find that after a number of years, you will become quite philosophical. You will see that what we at first perceive as a bad thing can turn out to have a very positive end. You will learn to go with the tide. When things are good, enjoy them to the utmost. When things are bad, endure them or do your best to change them. Remember that your will power is your ultimate strength. The cards are a useful tool in guiding you, but you are the master or mistress of your fate.

You will notice in the examples for the last card, the meanings are only given for the picture in position 1. This is because in the long run only the final result was important.

Sample Reading 1

January 12, 1980

Reading done for a married man with two children. The reading was done two days before he was fired unexpectedly.

38 LADY—position 4—Having sucked you dry, they will turn away from you.

35 ANCHOR—position 1—Success in love; you are loved.

3 SHIP—position 4—Material loss or unsuccessful efforts.

22 ROAD—position 3—A lonely and boring road or work.

8 HEARSE—position 4—You will escape danger in time.

13 BOY—position 4—An unexpected meeting or a date.

25 RING—position 2—Engagement to a rich person.

174

10 SCYTHE—position 2—You will hear a threat that will have consequences.

12 BIRDS—position 3—You expect someone not to fulfill a promise and you will be right.

LAST CARD: 45 PIG—position 1—Positively a prosperous and happy year.

48 ROOSTER—position 1—Soon you will hear good news.

50 BREAD—position 1—You will be made happy with a present.

37 ANGEL—position 1—A bright, wished-for happiness awaits you.

SUMMARY: A lot of negative pictures came up, warning of an impending misfortune, which was the firing. However, there were also positive pictures such as the RING and ANCHOR. These referred to the wife of the man, who loved and supported him throughout the ordeal. The last card, which predicts the final outcome, was very positive. The man lost his job, but he was able to reach a good severance settlement. Today he has a much better and more satisfying job. The cards predicted that trouble would come, but they also reminded him that he was loved, and that the final outcome would be good.

Sample Reading 2

January 12, 1980

Reading done for the wife of the man who was unexpectedly fired.

3 SHIP—position 1—You will receive an inheritance or a winning.

19 CASTLE—position 3—A long life.

25 RING—position 2—Engagement to a rich person.

27 LETTER—position 2—Interesting, unexpected news.

1 CAVALIER—position 4—Unpleasant news.

32 MOON—position 4—Delay in action will give a minus.

14 FOX—position 1—You are being cunningly deceived.

LAST CARD: 37 ANGEL—position 1—A bright, wished-for happiness awaits you.

45 PIG—position 1—Positively a prosperous and happy year.

48 ROOSTER—position 1—Soon you will hear good news.

50 BREAD—position 1—You will be made happy with a present.

SUMMARY: The wife did not receive the negative pictures that her husband did. She was starting a new career and many of the pictures referred to it. However, she was warned that she was being deceived. Her husband had not told her of the problems he was having at work. The bad news was that he was fired, and their security looked threatened. It is interesting that the last card came out the same for both of them. This usually does not happen to a husband and wife, but in this case they were both affected by the events and the final outcome was the same for both of them. The severance payment paid for their mortgage, while her salary was adequate to support them. The year that began with a calamity ended quite prosperously and happily.

Sample Reading 3

January 15, 1980

Reading done for the same man as in sample reading 1, the day after he was fired. The question he asked was, "What can I do now?"

20 FOREST—position 2—Mixing with a purpose in numerous and agreeable society.

26 BOOK—position 3—A secret entrusted to you will be disclosed.

19 CASTLE—position 4—A chronic illness.

176

5 FIREWOOD—position 4—A bruise, cut, or illness.

17 HERON—position 2—Circumstances will force you to enter an undesirable path.

LAST CARD: 15 BEAR—position 1—With caution, happiness will not elude you.
29 MONEY—position 1—You will receive a substantial sum of money.
23 MICE—position 1—You will find what you have lost.
2 CLOVER—position 1—Happiness and fulfillment of desires.

SUMMARY: Having lost his job unexpectedly after ten years of working, the man felt his situation was desperate. The CASTLE and FIREWOOD pictures warned of health problems resulting from the shock. The HERON picture indicated that just as the heron has to move to new territory when the fish in the stream are gone, so the man had to begin looking for new areas of work. However, no matter how hopeless the situation seems at the moment, the cards always point out how to achieve success in the circumstances. The FOREST picture indicated that the man should not withdraw at the moment, but should seek the company of his friends and acquaintances. He obtained good advice from his friend, a lawyer, and received a good severance payment. When he found work it was due to a friend's letting him know that a position was becoming available. The BEAR picture showed strength. There had to be sorrow at losing a job. Yet, by being careful, working on the positive rather than the negative, the man eventually was able to find a job more suited to his needs.

Sample Reading 4

May 20, 1982
This reading was done for a woman who was afraid her husband was having an affair.

26 BOOK—position 4—Your talkativeness will bring you harm.

177

43 CRAYFISH—position 4—Too much haste often defeats the business.

34 OWL—position 1—At the present time you want to act unwisely.

19 CASTLE—position 3—A long life.

48 ROOSTER—position 1—Soon you will hear good news.

41 CAT—position 3—Having received a blow, you will hide your feelings with dignity.

38 LADY—position 2—The helping hand is given to you not in friendship but due to hidden love.

1 CAVALIER—position 1—You will hear pleasant news.

35 ANCHOR—position—Disillusionment with the ideal; doubts.

LAST CARD: 21 MOUNTAINS—position 1—A treacherous enemy is trying to catch you; be on guard.

14 FOX—position 1—You are being cunningly deceived.

7 SNAKE—position 1—A verbal sting by a malicious person.

9 BOUQUET—position 1—Great success in all affairs.

SUMMARY: The picture confirmed the woman's suspicions that her husband was being unfaithful to her. However, there was a caution not to rush into things and a warning that haste and talkativeness would bring problems. Surprisingly, the RING, HANDSHAKE, KNOT, and BRANCHES pictures did not come up. These pictures can signal the end of a relationship. The pictures did indicate that strong friends would support her and that she would have great success. The woman was able to work out the problems with her husband. Today they are still married and quite happy.

Sample Reading 5

June 7, 1979

This reading was done for a woman whose husband had quit his secure job to accept a post with U.N.E.S.C.O. in a Third World country.

23 MICE—position 2—An unexpected discovery.

44 FIRE—position 4—You will be warmed by love during difficult, cold days.

27 LETTER—position 1—Happiness will come to you from far away.

25 RING—position 2—Engagement to a rich person.

49 DAGGER—position 3—You will experience a prick to your pride.

LAST CARD: 42 SCALES—position 1—In your fate, good will out-weigh evil.
29 MONEY—position 1—You will receive a substantial sum of money.
34 OWL—position 1—At the present time you want to act unwisely.
39 HORSE—position 1—You will experience a vivid or traumatic life event.

SUMMARY: This was an emotionally turbulent time for the woman. She was hurt and surprised at her husband's sudden decision. She was also excited at the prospect of going to a Third World country. There were many decisions for her to make. The cards warned her to be careful in all her dealings. Her fear at the loss of a secure salary were answered by both the RING and MONEY pictures. Both pictures assured her that there should be no worries about money. The surprising picture was the FIRE. She was going to a tropical country, so why was she going to be warmed by love during difficult, cold days? Several years later, when the family returned, the question had been answered. Along with the beauty of the country, she had witnessed poverty and the bleakness the population faced. It was the love of her own family that made it bearable for her to witness the troubling things.

Sample Reading 6

November 7, 1987
    This reading was done for a man on the night before a strike at his place of employment.

179

7 SNAKE—position 2—Betrayal, unfaithfulness

15 BEAR—position 3—You will get what you desire although not in the immediate future.

6 APPLE—position 3—An unpleasant meeting, encounter.

43 CRAYFISH—position 2—Your pride will be hurt.

42 SCALES—position 3—If you maintain your balance, you will come out whole from a predicament.

30 LILY—position 4—Useless doubts about faithfulness; jealousy.

20 FOREST—position 2—Mixing with a purpose in numerous and agreeable society.

LAST CARD: 16 STARS—position 1—Your guiding star will bring you to your goal.
33 FISH—position 1—Fortune, especially on the sea.
12 BIRDS—position 1—Joy, merriment.
25 RING—position 1—A wedding or agreement.

SUMMARY: The man was in an unsettling position. He supported the policy of his company, yet most of his good friends opposed it. The reading helped him decide to follow his gut instinct, which was to stand for his principles. He saw that by crossing the picket line, he would have an unpleasant encounter, and his pride would be hurt. The SNAKE picture showed that either he or his friends would feel betrayed. Nevertheless, there were enough positive pictures to encourage him to stand his ground. The FOREST picture indicated that his friends would remain friends after the ordeal. The last card showed the outcome of the situation. All four pictures were positive, indicating ultimate success. The SCALES picture warned him to use his common sense. By sticking to his principles and respecting the principles of others, he was able to maintain friendly relations. It is also interesting that the cards showed that during this difficult ordeal, he would get closer to his wife. The cards always refer not only to the situation you are concerned about, but also to surrounding forces you may not be aware of.

Sample Reading 7

January 19, 1987
This reading was done for myself on the day when it is customary to do a reading for the year.

45 PIG—position 4—Overindulgence in food will make you sick.

 9 BOUQUET—position 4—You will find a means of earning money.

46 BRIDGE—position 1—A radical change in lifestyle awaits you.

20 FOREST—position 3—Contact with suspicious people.

28 HORSESHOE—position 2—Everything that you undertake in the near future will be successful.

32 MOON—position 4—Delay in action will work against you.

 2 CLOVER—position 2—Happiness slightly clouded by a misunderstanding.

LAST CARD: 19 CASTLE—position 1—Fulfillment of hopes, although at the end of your life.
18 DOG 1—You have a faithful and constant friend.
34 OWL—position 1—At the present time you want to act unwisely.
42 SCALES—position 1—In your fate, good will outweigh evil.

SUMMARY: The reading was somewhat disappointing. I was hoping that the cards would indicate that this would be a good year to finish working on translating the cards and writing this book. The OWL and the CASTLE pictures showed that the time was not right. Other things concerning my family needed attention. However, the CASTLE did indicate that my desires would get fulfilled, although at the end of my life; therefore, I should enjoy my life at the moment.

Interesting additional advice was shown by the FOREST picture. Shortly after the reading, two students in my class began harassing their fellow classmates and me. These were not mischievous pranks but malicious acts. The picture had been a warning to me. The SCALES picture also gave good advice. By maintaining my balance and

181

not overreacting, I was able to get the problem resolved somewhat. The boys were asked to leave the school. However, the FOREST picture kept coming up for almost a year, warning me of potential danger. I was also reassured by the SCALES picture in position 1; good would outweigh evil in my future.

Sample Reading 8

September 3, 1989
  Reading done for myself. My question was, "What lies ahead?"

46 BRIDGE—position 1—A radical change in lifestyle awaits you.

11 BRANCHES—position 3—A breakup with a close person.

31 SUN—position 1—Prosperity, flourishment, life's caress, happiness.

23 MICE—position 1—You will find what you have lost.

43 CRAYFISH—position 3—Delay is sometimes designed by fate.

47 DEMONS—position 4—Your fervor will not lead to any good.

26 BOOK—position 3—A secret entrusted to you will be disclosed.

35 ANCHOR—position 2—Fulfillment of hopes; success on the sea.

LAST CARD: 25 RING—position 1—A wedding or agreement.
        33 FISH—position 1—Fortune, especially on the sea.
        16 STARS—position 1—Your guiding star will bring
            you to your goal.
        12 BIRDS—position 1—Joy, merriment.

SUMMARY: This was a most welcome reading. I had given up my teaching job to work on this book. The ANCHOR, FISH, and STARS pictures all indicated that what I was doing was correct for me. There was a definite change in lifestyle, from being a teacher to a writer. My time was no longer fragmented by bell schedules and student questions. What I had wished for for so long was finally coming into being. The BRANCHES indicated my son leaving for college. Rather than being sad, I realized that it gave me more time to work. The SUN picture, my favorite, and the BIRDS picture reflected the joy that I was feeling at the moment. This was my time to do what I wanted.

182